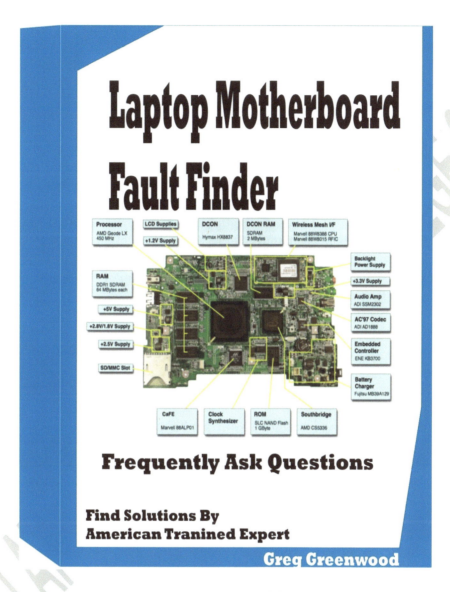

# All Rights Reserved

# Introduction

**Before You Start**

As a Laptop technician, you must understand a basic rule of business, time is money. Whether you are boss or work for someone else, the ability to identify and isolate a Laptop fault quickly and decisively is very important to the success of your business. It requires some common sense, and a little bit of focus. It also requires an understanding of the troubleshooting process, and reliable plan of action. Even though the number of Laptop configuration and setups are virtually unlimited, the methodology used to approach each repair is always about the same. This introduction is intended to isolate the concepts of basic troubleshooting and show you how to apply basic laptop repair steps that will help you narrow the problem down before you even take a screwdriver to the Laptop. By applying a constant technique. You can safe precious time from every laptop repair.

**The General Troubleshooting Steps**

Regardless of how your particular Laptop might be, a dependable Troubleshooting steps can be broken down into four basic steps.
**#1:Define your symptoms,**
**#2: identify and isolate the location of your problem**
**#3: replace the suspected component, and**
**#4:re-test the component thoroughly to be sure that you have solve the problem.**
If you have not solved the problem, start again from step #1:This is a "universal" procedure that you can apply to any sort of troubleshooting __not just for Laptops.

**DEFINE YOUR SYMPTOMS**

When a Laptop breaks down, the cause might be a simple as a loose wire or a connector, or as complicated as an IC or component failure. Before you start, you must have a good understanding of all the symptoms. Think about the symptoms carefully. By recognizing and understanding your symptoms, it can be much easier to trace a problem to the appropriate component. Take the time to write down as many symptoms as you can. As a Laptop technician, you must often write problems and solutions for reference purposes.

**IDENTIFY AND ISOLATE**

Before you try to isolate a problem within a piece of Laptop hardware, you must first be sure that the equipment itself is causing the problem. In many cases, this will be fairly obvious, but some situation might not be. A faulty or improperly configured piece of software can cause confusing system errors. When you are sure that it is a system's hardware failure, you can begin to identify which component fails.

**REPLACE**

Because Laptops are designed as a sub-unit, it is almost always easier to replace a sub-unit outright, rather than attempt to repair the sub-unit to its component level. Even if you had the time, to isolate defective component, many laptop parts are not inter-changeable, so it is better to replace the defective part than try to repair it

**RE-TEST**

When a repair is finally complete, the system must be reassembly carefully before testing it. All guards, housings, cables and shields must replaced before final testing. If symptoms persist, you will have to reevaluate the symptoms and narrow the problem to another parts of the equipment. If normal operation is restored (or greatly improved), test the computer's various function. When you can verify that the symptoms have stop during actual operation, the equipment can be returned to service. As a general rule, it is wise to let the system run for at least 24 hours to ensure that the replacement sub-assembly will not fail prematurely.

Do not be discouraged if the equipment still malfunctions. Maybe software settings and device drivers may need to be updated to. If you are tired simply walk away, clear your hand, and start again by defining the current symptoms. Never continue with a repair if you are tired or frustrated tomorrow is another day. Even the most experienced troubleshooters get overwhelmed from time to time.

# Problem: 001

**What are common faults on mainboards?**

**Do certain components fail? Is there a trend as to which parts fail quite often?**

# Solution:

Different maker/model has different common fault. Toshiba S1 is vga chip, and can't be

repaired(well, almost can't be repaired because the pcb quality is not very good so

successful rate is very low).

HP DV2000, 6000, 9000, compaq v3000, v6000, dell 1210, all those use nvidia chips have

problem on vga chip or north bridge. easy to repair but have to make fan keep spinning after

repaired, otherwise will break down in 1 or 2 week again.

hp nx5000, cpu pwm chip dry joint. acer 290, cpu pwm dry joint.

hp dv1000, compaq m2000 protection circuit easy to blow up.

ibm t40 vga dry joint problem.

These are just few of them. every machine has its own common fault. but dry joint is the

common problem for all machines.

repair mobo is not as difficult as people thought, i think much easer than repair a tv.

yesterday i fix an acer 4600 and take only about 15min.

the machine wont turn on when customer bring in.

1. plug in our power supply and it shows short circuit on board, the current jump to the 5A,

which is the limit of my power supply.
2. take off the mobo, drop the voltage of power supply to 5v, limit current to about 1A, plug

in again and find a mos very hot.
3. replace this mos, now the short circuit fixed.
4. turn on, the current goes up to 0.3A and stopped, it should go up to 1A during booting.
5. touch cpu, not hot, no power to cpu.
6. check the cpu pwm, which is max1907a. all conditions to make it work are present, but

still no power output. the ref voltage is 0. so most likely this chip gone.
7. replace the chip and everything work fine.


# Problem:002


**Compaq v3118au. the integrated nv6150 overheats during this freezing winter usually goes to**

**about 105 deg c before it thermally shutdowns (and this is even after just watching youtube**

**videos).. and sometimes if you turn the laptop on straight after this.. it won't even turn on or it'll boot straight into a BSOD with a message saying "video driver failed to initialize".**

## Solution:

To fix such machine, first you have to do bga reworking on the chip, then connect fan to usb power to make it spin faster and non stop. also need to cut off fan controling wire.

HP DV2000, 6000, 9000, compaq v3000, v6000, dell 1210, all those use nvidia chips have problem on vga chip or north bridge. easy to repair but have to make fan keep spinning after repaired, otherwise will break down in 1 or 2 week again.

# Problem:003

**Are you able to replace the graphics card on a dell 1420, the gfx card is a nvidia 8400gs**

## Solution:

Replacing the vga chip is the only way to fix it. Because it involves bga reworking and bga reworking involve high risk to destroy pcb.

# Problem:004

**My D505 may power on boot OK or may have following condition.**
**a)LED flash**
**b)"da.da.da....." sound.**

## Solution:

If you know the bios manufacturer, the beep code will tell you where the failure is.

So the number of beeps and the duration of each beep is a specific code from the bios to let you know what it couldn't start – like video, memory, cpu etc.

# Problem:005

**Toshiba Satellite A205-SP4077, Core 2 Duo. While replacing cracked LCD tried several panels with no success. Then noticed LVDS RX2- signal from motherboard is missing.**

## Solution:

It is the north bridge dry joint, it is common fault of this model. Do BGA reworking on

north bridge, and replace the north bridge if bga reworking doesn't work.

# Problem: 006

**Machine: HP G6000(same mainboard as V6000)**

**Laptop will not power up**

**The machine has been water damaged. It does not have system standby power, which are 3V and**

**5V.**

## Solution:

Check Max8724(the battery charging chip) first, because to make system has standby power

this chip must work correctly. This is a 28 pin chip, we only need to test 1, 2, 4, 8, 10,

11 pin. They are VIN(main power for chip), LDO(provide 3.3V for chip itself in order to set

REF voltage, also provide signal to drive 2 MOS to charge battery), REF(set reference

voltage of the chip), SHDN#(enable/disable chip, a switch), ACIN(indicate the power supply

has plugged in), ACOK#(power adaptor ok with mainboard).

Everything ok except 10 pin, ACIN is 0V. This is incorrect, mainboard doesn't detect there

is an adaptor! Trace it backward and find it is very simple – mainboard use 2 resistors to

pull the input voltage(19V, directly from dc socket) down to about 4V, so test the first

resistor and find it opened. Change it and 3V/5V power come up and mainboard be able to

switch on.

Then the trouble start when I try to charge the battery. The charging current never go

beyond 0.15A and after 10 seconds the charging light start to flashing. Also can't switch on

from battery. First, change Max8724, still same problem. Next check all the resistors around

max8724 and change it if it has any sign of watering, still no good. Then change

KB3926(EC/KBC, chip monitors the statue of battery), still same. This is the fault that I

never dealt with before.

Decide to check MBDATA and MBCLCK, 2 signals that send battery information from battery to

KB3926 before I give up. I find the MBDATA is short!

Finally, find there are 2 pins stick together on CN10(the connector of multimedia switch

board). Fix it and it start to charging battery. Switch on with power adaptor, ok. Remove

the power adaptor once switch on, battery keep the mainboard running, ok. But still can't

switch on from battery once remove the power adaptor. Think, think, do I miss something here

or there? Oh, the CMOS battery not installed, put the CMOS battery back and everything work

perfectly. The battery part of troubleshooting takes me about 3 hours.

Remember, system may not run if you don't have CMOS battery or CMOS battery is low for some

AMD cpu mainboard.

## Question:

what is "dry joint"?

## Answer:

Shortened version of 'dry solder joint'.
http://www.electronics-tutorials.com/basics/soldering.htm

Look at the 'common faults' area.

# Problem:007

My friend bought Lenovo g530 c2d t6500 and the lower part of the screen get hot (not overheating) , he was wondering if that normal or this is hardware issue?

## Solution:

It is normal as long as it is not overheating.

# Problem:008

Are you able to give some general advice about keyboards? A friend has an Acer, one of the alphabetic keytops has come off

## Solution:

First, put the retainer(or what you said "hinge") onto the keyboard base, then put the key

on the top, slightly press down and lock the key on the retainer.

# Problem:009

I have problem with Toshiba S1900-102.

I bought a new battery about 5 months ago, then the laptop did not work on battery and it's still at 35% and did not charge any more.

so I bought a used battery, and when I first connect it, plug the power cable and turn on the laptop, I open Windows Power Meter. it's work and begin charging till 60%, so I want to try it I unplugged power cable and the laptop still works, and when I plug the power cable again the Power Meter status said: AC Power. not charging I unplugged the power cable and the laptop turn off

I disassembled the battery to see what going on inside, I see M37516M6 microcomputer with a white shade around it.

Note: the second Battery still at 60% charge and didn't increase or decrease

## Solution:

Most end users have no means to test battery. We test battery by monitoring the charging current. The battery is ok if we see the charging current goes up, say to over 1A and hold for a while. To check the battery condition, we firstly run the battery flat. Plug the power supply which has current meter, see how long the charging current drop to normal standby current. If we see it just take 30 min to drop to standby current, the battery may only last 10 min during normal usage.

In your case, I could not say what is wrong because I have to see if there is charging current.

## Tech Secret:

For lots of unknown brand laptops, sometimes very hard to find drivers. I don't know how many people know there is a trick to install a similar driver.

Machine: TPG (can't see the model clearly)

Could not find the driver, TPG web site only point to Asus web site and doesn't give which model it clone from Asus. We can't find vga driver.

We use Everest to check what vga chip it use and find it is ATI IGP 320M U1. Download few from different web sites, all of them just give a message said could not find hardware it supports.

Finally, download a driver from fujitsu web site for the lifebook S2020(same vga chip and south bridge chip as TPG's). But still give the error message said no support hardware find.

Every device has a Device Instance ID, and windows will compare this ID with driver's INF. It will install the driver if it find a match ID and match SubSys, otherwise will give an error message.

We check the driver for S2020, find the string "PCI\VEN_1002&DEV_4336&SUBSYS_118110CF" in one of the INF file. We also find the Device ID on our machine is "PCI\VEN_1002&DEV_4336&SUBSYS_2029161F&REV_00". Device ID is matched but just into different sub system. Replace the string in S2020's INF with our Device ID string, driver is installed correctly and no error message.

# Problem:010

I currently have a HP DV6000 sitting in front of me with several rows of black/grey lines over the screen. Is it worth trying to fix yourself or should I just send it in for a warranty repair

## Solution:

Send for warranty if it is still in warranty. Otherwise, forget it. not worth to repair. To complete solve this problem, you need to replace Nvidia chip which was made after 30th week of 08. The chips are very hard to source, all chips go to manufactories and I have waited for more than 3 month but still not get my order filled.

# Problem:011

**A friend opened up his notebook to give it a clean but when he put it back together the bios is not finding the hard drive**

## Solution:

Make sure you plug hard disk firmly.

It could be the problem of south bridge, the south bridge controls hdd. I have seen many times  that clean cpu fan and end up with non working laptop.

# Problem:012

**I've got a stuffed Toshiba Satellite A100 I'm trying to diagnose at the moment.**

## Solution:

A100 as series has many different version, I don't know which one you have. I just tell you the common problems of this model.

First, it does not power up at all. The charging light flashes and nothing on the screen. I am still trying to find out what faulty of such kind.

Second, it powers up but nothing on the screen. The power up sequence of working machine is like: 0.2A – 1.0A – 0.75A – 0.9A – 1.2A. Most time the faulty machines will stop at 1.0A or 0.75A, the cpu is not hot. In such case, the North Bridge does not send cpu rst signal to do hardware reset. So this is north bridge problem.

Third, it only run on one memory.

This is also north bridge problem.

# Problem:013

**I swapped fans on my old Thinkpad (T40) the other day: fan is fine now, but nothing else works, not even a flashing cursor on the screen, so the BIOS hasn't started.**

**Any suggestions about where to proceed from here?**

## Solution:

The common problem of this model is vga chip dry joint. check the hdd light flashing or not, it should be the vga if it flashes.

# Problem:014

**Toshiba tecra M9 dropped, worked for a few days and then died.**

**no HDD activity, the backlight doesn't turn on and the screen shows nothing.**

## Solution:

The hardest repair laptop is dropped one, even harder than watering. The south bridge, north bridge and vga chip all could be dry joint. To fix such machine, I always resolder those big chips, sometimes it works and sometimes it is not. There is no good way to fix such machines, just simply take the chance.

# Problem:015

**Do you think if I heat up the VGA chip (or SB or NB) then the solder will melt and get fixed?**

**If so, what should I use to heat it up?**

## Solution:

I am not suggesting you do that unless you have bga rework station. The temperature control must be very strictly. But if you want to take the chance, I suggest you use 2 hot air guns, one from top, one from bottom. Set the top temperature to 350, set the bottom to 300 and blow it about 10 min.

To be honest with you, I have less than 10% successful rate for dropped machines even I have a bga rework station. The watering boards I have more than 70% successful rate.

In the case you want to go ahead with such project. you must firmly fix both air guns and motherboard, not let them move when you blow the hot air. Use a little stick to touch the capacitors or resistors around the big chips, keep blowing about 5 min when the solder on

small components reflowed. Don't forget to apply flux between big chips and pcb board. don't

set bottom temperature too high, otherwise the components on the bottom may fall off. Good

luck.

# Problem:016

**Acer Travelmate 3260 (bought 2007), the power input pin has broken and it no longer gets any power to the system.**

**Do you have the schematic for this model and also do you have instruction on how to replace**

**the power socket, plus where to buy the component from?**

## Solution:

You don't really need schematic for such repair job. The DC jack you can find on ebay, I

think someone in uk sell all type of jack. you also can attach a cable if you couldn't find

such jack, and such connector can be easily found in ebay.

# Problem:017

**HP pavilion dv5-1010tx**

**1) The computer overheats REALLY easily now**

**2) I use dual screens (laptop screen + Benq E2200HD via HDMI) and the external monitor will**

**occasionally flick. (every 10-15 seconds it will go black for half a second)**

## Solution:

Yes, that is overload to vga chip.

I still remember that back about 3 years ago I saw people modified their IBM Thinkpad, they use QXGA(resolution is 2048x1536) to replace original sxga(1400x900). The result of doing

this is vga chip get overheat and kill machine fast, usually not over one year. But for the

people can do such modify is no problem to fix their motherboard – resolder the vga chip, or

replace vga chip.

The more calculation of vga chip carried, the more heat it generated. Think about how many

calculation jobs that vga chip has to do in your situation, not only the internal lcd, but

also the external lcd. Much more than those people change lcd from sxga to qxga.

# Problem:018

 **Its ASUS F3SC**

**Mums laptop has crashed and when you boot, the screen is split so there are 2 identical
screens vertically (1 above the other). It wont boot normally or last good config but will
boot safely with networking but if it boots like this, wouldn't that suggest a hardware/bios
issue.**

## Solution:

This is not a bios issue, First swap the lcd with a know good working one to in order to rule out lcd problem
if problem continue then reflow or reball the gpu to fix the problem.

# Problem:019

 **I heated up the CPU.**

**I still have the same result**

## Solution:

 The first step to troubleshooting is monitor the current change. Usually, current reading  can tell you what was
wrong and quite accurate.

CPU faulty is rarely happened. I only see no more than 5 to 8 cpu faulty during 10 years.

CPU kills motherboard happen on me once, and that motherboard in turn to kill another good

CPU, and this is p3 cpu.

Don't worry about cpu, 99% chance it is good.

Try to do this, find a current meter, cut off the wire of power adapter, and connect current

meter to the wire. The meter must be able to read at least 0.01A.

# Problem:020

I have a Toshiba Tecra A9 that is out of warranty but has a faulty Ethernet, i.e. it never

see's that it is plugged in. Thinking that it was a dry joint I opened it up to find that

the Ethernet port is connected to the motherboard via a cable, so I re-seated the plug but

it still doesn't work. The cable is still "unplugged" according to the OS (both Windows and

Linux), the interface is detected in the OS and appears to be working fine, just no plugged

in if you know what I mean.

Do you have any advice to troubleshoot this issues? Other than the Ethernet issues the

machines works fine.

## Solution:

So is it all 8 wires running from the Ethernet connector to the mainboard connector ?
If so then maybe you can just re-wire it.

Get a spare Ethernet cable and cut a piece to size. Then just join it to the connectors.

(You might need to get a tool for this, but they can be found at DSE and places like that)
Ethernet cables are generally color coded so you should be able to re-wire it easily.

OR try this easy method below.

When an Ethernet (LAN) port goes on a laptop, the best thing I feel to do is just go and buy a PCMCIA card (this laptop will have one) where you can either buy new or online for second hand. You might even find one at your local garage sales which will cost you next to nothing. All you need to do is look up on the net for the drivers and away you go.
Please note that you will only get 10/100 base speed with these cards.

# Problem:021

I have a working Dell inspiron 630m with no screen ( was 14" ) and a bricked NEC Versa m540

15" screen. The screen on the nec would still work but the bios was flashed and took out the

bios chip and MOBO. So I have the brains of the dell and the sight of the nec. Is there any

issue with voltage and connectivity between the dell and the nec screen if I take both apart

and try to merge the two.

# Solution:

The screens are unlikely to be compatible.

Even if the same internal connector is used.
Internal LCD screens use a bunch of differential signals and different signal timing and

structure for different screens.

Some different Model Dells do use same screen. It would be easier to use an LCD external

monitor of correct size and fit it to the Dell frame and run VGA cable to it.

# Problem:022

I have tried to find an answer to this question on google, but never can.
I have a alienware m17x.
i was playing, when the computer suddenly reset.
When it reset, it had problems detecting my 2 video cards gtx-280m in sli

i reinstall driver, and the card were detected. Nvidia control panel says it is running SLI,

but from benchmarking and playing games i get huge FPS lag.

## Solution:

Please  turn off your power off, take out the battery, unplug AC power and press the power

on for 30 seconds. and then  turn laptop back on, The laptop should work.  It is called

power laptop draining.

# Problem:023

Week ago a customer brought me a dell inspiron 6400 with a power problem.

Laptop can't run nor charge the battery on adapter, but on battery it's run.

the problem was due to incorrect adapter connected to it.

so any idea for what happened in it

## Solution:

This is typical circuit protection problem. check the 2 mosfet just after power socket.

# Problem:024

I am thinking of installing a new Seagate Momentus 7200.4 hard drive in my sony vaio FW46.

Does anyone know whether this computer supports SATA 3.0gb/s interface? If so, do I need to

adjust any settings before or after installation?

## Solution:

sony vaio FW46 can do it, drop it in and install windows. nothing needed to tweak in bios.

# Problem:025

 I have been repairing HpDVxxxx laptop with the video problem for a few years and have

gotten very good at reballing/replacing the chip. I am now trying to figure out the NO power

at all or wont charge the battery EX Compaq C700 I have about 50 of these laptops will run

on good battery windows shows it is charging the battery screen gets bright when you plug in

the ac charger goes dimm when you unplug it but it will not charge. I would like to know

what chip to start with I also have several DV9000 and dv6000 MB that do not get any power

at all. Any help on what chips to look at would be great.

## Solution:

C700's charging chip is 39A126, DV6000/9000's charging chip is max8724 or max8725. Check the

working conditions of those chips. such as VIN, ACIN, ACOK, LDO, REF, SHDN.

Charging problem is second hardest problem on notebook repairing, the first one is signal

level – everything looks ok but just no display.

# Problem:026

Anyone had any luck repairing a Dell 1525 Inspiron that says system does not recognize the

installed batter this system will not charge the battery.
It is a new actual Dell battery and charger. It is not the dc jack it i sthe chip that is on

the motherboard. I have a lot of these and I have had no luck fixing them and have sent them

out to several other places and they say that once that chip goes it can not be repaired (no

one has the info to program on the chip for it to work correctly???) I think there should be

a bios mod that will do away with this check and it would work???? Just seems a waste of

good laptops as they all work some you get lucky and they see the ac charger and will run on

that others will not see any charger but do see the battery once it is dead no more using

the laptop. I can get stand alone chargers but that is a pain to do.

Also wondering if it is possible to solder wires from the DC jack on the motherboard to the

battery contacts if this would charge the battery and bypass the motherboard?? Have not

tried this yet as I do not want to burn the place down.

I think the bios mod is the way to go. just seeing if anyone has repair this.

## Solution:

Charging battery in Dell laptop involves two major chips: EC(or someone call it super IO),

PWM chip for battery charging. BIOS has no part of charging. Battery communicate with EC

through SMB(system management bus??) and EC controls charging PWM. Fix charging problem is

very hard in laptop repair, you must fully understand schematics – where all the signals

come from and where to go.

Today's laptops are less and less with programmed EC, Dell 1525 has no programmed EC so it

can be replaced with same model.

# Problem:027

I would like to repair a system board in a compaq M2217AP (EE504PA) laptop. I believe the protection circuit has failed and with my basic knowledge of electronics have located the failed component. I require a copy of the circuit diagram or if you aren't able to supply, a correct identification for part PC75. Can you assist?

## Solution:

PC75 is a capacitor, which is on the main power circuit. Luckily I have a such board in hand, and I have checked where is the PC75 already. don't worry about this capacitor, just take it off if you think it is faulty. Pay attention to PQ24, PQ26, PQ25, PC68-70, PC16-19, PC48, PC45, PC35, PC110-112. There is a guideline in here, all these components are located on main power. There is also a guide when you check – check all the inductors and make sure they are not short.

# Problem:028

I had a working Lenovo T500 with switchable graphics (discrete/integrated). While swapping out the CPU for a more powerful one (P9700), I didn't realise that I knocked the modem cable, which slipped under the heat sink and onto the surface of the discrete GPU (ATI Radeon HD3650). This GPU has some sort of black heat shield covering on the surface edge. On restart, it booted to Win 7, before panicking into a NMI Parity error blue screen.

Quickly identifying the issue, I restored it, but now I am not able to switch graphics.

In the BIOS, it's set to 'Switchable'. If I select it to be either 'Discrete' or

'Integrated' it boots, but black screens and halts seconds after boot (no BIOS welcome screen). I can only restore the BIOS config by removing the internal backup battery.

If I leave it on 'Switchable' it boots into Win7, but it's using the 'Integrated' drivers.

Using the Lenovo switchable graphics drivers/mode, it runs something, but nothing happens to the screen... (in the past, it blacked out briefly and switched).

Is there anyway of fixing this without replacing the entire motherboard? I checked on the Lenovo site, and it's $700-$900? Which section of the MB do I inspect to see if I have damaged how the 'Switchable' graphics is controlled? Any other diagnostics tips?

## Solution:

First, get another hdd and install os again, eliminate software issue. If software has no problem, then the ATI chip may have been damaged. I never fix such problem before so I have no idea where to start. I will change the vga chip first if I have a such motherboard, but maybe only 50% chance to solve the problem by doing this – and doing bga on vga has risk – not really good option.

## Problem:029

I have an IBM T42 thinkpad (1400 x 1050, ATI chip) with some vertical lines on the screen. From what others have said, the chip might need to be reflowed (does that sound right?) The laptop is working fine otherwise and is such a great machine (I like it more than my kitted out work laptop – an i7 X201 with SSD). I'd love to get it fixed but want to know what kind of risk is involved in such a repair? Do you think its worth it? The lines are annoying but not bad enough that I'd risk bricking it if the repair was tricky.

## Solution:

Yes, reflowing will fix the problem but sometimes last for more than a year and sometimes

may only last for few weeks. To be last longer, you must take the vga chip off from

motherboard, reballing and solder it back.

The risk is for inexperience tech may totally kill the motherboard, especially if the tech

don't have right equipment..

# Problem:030

**I don't know if this is a stupid question but, are there many problems with netbooks? Have**

**you fixed many of them? Is there anything in particular to look out for?**

## Solution:

I haven't repaired many netbooks, I think because it is too cheap so people throw it away

once it was broken. The particular thing to look out is not the thing that can be controlled

by users. Ok, many people don't know why notebooks broken down so often, there are 3

reasons:

1. bad working conditions, from what i can see the working condition of laptop just a little

better than the things work in outspace. heat, dust, etc.
2. immature technology, the lead free soldering still in its developing stage. lots of

problems are not resolved yet. In the options of save the environment or save your laptop,

government regulations say save the environment first.
3. every manufactory try to cut the cost, so the quality and quantity of components they  use...

# Problem:031

i have also problem with HP NX7400, it starts up but no output on the monitor, sometimes when i shake the monitor a little the LCD work, i tried to connect external monitor but it didn't work, so i'm confused is it VGA chip problem or another problem in the M.B?.

## Solution:

The problem is the data cable between the motherboard and the LCD, open the lcd panel reattach the data cable firmly to the lcd screen and also the motherboard.

# Problem:032

The problem of machine is cannot power up at all.

## Solution:

Doing routine check:

1. system power: 3V, 5V all presented -ok
2. NBSWON signal: 3.3V presented – ok
3. press power button, NBSWON pull down to 0V, ok
4. check DNBSWON while press power button, no response. – problem.
in here I made a mistake, I didn't pay attention of the voltage of DNBSWON, this mistake

waste me the next few days time. It should be 3.3V, but only about 1V.

Change EC as usual, because I thought the EC has problem. Then the big trouble comes – it

auto power up once I plug in the power but stop in 0.04A current. Check and find no S5_ON

signal, which indicate south bridge has problem, so change south bridge. But still same

problem and still no S5_ON. I was going to give up. I take a close look before I call

customer to say need to change motherboard, and I find that the EC I change is kb3926A

rather than kb3926C. In most case, this is no problem but in very rare occation...

So I find a 3926C and put on. Now the motherboard is back to the same problem while I first start to check! So I change a wrong EC and this time I change a correct one, and also EC has

no problem!

Because EC will start to read bios once the power plug in(not as people think, once you

press power button). I check BIOS chip, BIOS_CS should have a countinue wave form but it

just one stright line. BIOS chip is faulty! Take me 3 days to find out. If I could think

more when I check DNBSWON, if I could checked BIOS_CS before I change EC, if I could

replaced with a kb3926c not kb3926a. This was one hour job but took me 3 days.

# Problem:033

Just wondering I have an acer laptop 5720z, with a problem, after a couple of hours the unit

becomes unresponsive, then a couple of minutes later it shuts down.

## Solution:

Have you tried to clean the heatsink and cooling fans? It seems like overheating.

# Problem:034

Compaq Presario CQ50 which  powers on but no boot. Power light comes on and HDD led blinks

Briefly.  No beeps or video. Current goes to about 1.0 A and then 1.6 A

## Solution:

 Replaced CPU.  It seems overheated.

# Problem:035

I live in the Netherlands and there are no good laptop repair centers available so I bought myself a T-862++ BGA SMB rework station. I allready fixed my own HP laptop.

But I am having trouble with a couple of acer notebooks I fixed in my spare time. Repair

works fine. Sadly I have had all 3 of them back in no time. I have done the repair same way

as on my own HP laptop. I guess it has something to do with the brand Acer? Or are my

settings wrong?

My settings in Fahrenheit are
Lower heating plate set at 392
This heats the pcb to a 212
Then I put on the top IR heater to get the chip temp at 392 degrees fahrenheit for just a

few seconds.   Any idea's?

## Solution:

For lead free solder, the melt temperature is 217c, solder contains lead is 183c. To do bga

on a lead free solder motherboard, you need 3 temp zones machine, 2 zones machine is not

enough and easy to damage motherboard.

My machine I set top nozzle to 270c, bottom nozzle to 230c, around heating plate 180c. I

keep heating the chip about 70sec after it reach to 270c. There is also few important

things:

1. temp raise not over 3c per sec.

2. keeping heating at least 20sec after chip can be moved.

3.use powerful fan to cool down the motherboard once heating process finished.

BTW, for lead free motherboard or chip reflow is meaningless, cos it may work for a while

and will stop working after few weeks. The chips must be taken off and reballing or change

a new chip. HP laptops like DV2000, DV6000 such are not really dry joint – or we should say

they are dry joint inside of chip, not from motherboard. So reflow can't solve the problem,

you have to change a new chip. Believe me, there is one trick we decide if the vga chips need to be changed or not for those no display machine, we use hot air gun set to 360c and blow the chips for about 10sec. After that if we see the display come up, then we know this chip is faulty.

few unsuccessful attempts are necessary to learn how to do bga reworking. I have burnt at least 8 or 9 boards one year ago while I change my old machine to current one, at that time I already had more than 3 years experience on bga reworking.

# Problem:036

**Have you repaired any Compaq C700 laptops that will not charge the battery or run off AC charger? You put in a charged battery and plug in the AC cord the blue light on the DC jack will light up it says it is charging windows will show as plugged in and charging. But it does not if you remove the battery it will turn off. Plug in the charger with the battery removed the Blue DC jack light will not come on. I have a stack of these that all do the same. I am just now getting some time to mess with them. This is what I have found so far.**

**Putting a jumper wire from the DC Jack + wire to the first battery fitting (far left with the laptop face down battery compartment away) this will let the computer run on the AC power cord with the battery removed. I had to compare readings to a DV6000 as none of my C700 will run on the Charger. The readings from a working DV6000 at the battery pins left to right are (plugged in NO battery)**

**0v 3.35v 3.35v 0v 3.35v 0v**

**Battery plugged in and plugged to charger**
**12.36v 3.35v 3.35v 0v 2.26v 0v**

**C700 with AC cord and jumper wire installed**

**19.2v 5.56v 3.35v 0v 4.26v 0v**

**I have not tried putting in the jumper wire with charger and battery I do not know if it**

would charge the battery or if it would blow up.

there are thousands of these with the same issue so it is most likely the same problem on

all of them just wondering if you have fixed any of these.

## Solution:

On the upper left right by where the DC jack plugs in there is a mosfet that on the working

board I get 19v on all 8 legs on the one with no power I get -.01v.

That is normal, it is a p channel mosfet – so control leg( the 4th pin) should be low

voltage. There is no power on m/b if you find this pin is high. But it also depend on the

verson of motherboard, with DV6000, some have n channel mosfet – in the case of N channel

mosfet the pin 4 must be high voltage. use p channel or n channel depends on protection

circuit. I can write you the info about how the power goes in and generate 3/5V system

standby power if you could tell me the motherboard project code.

## Problem:037

**No power on at all on some DV6000 motherboards.**

**Motherboard test readings**

**Dv6000 no power voltage test on good working board listed first then voltage on non working board.**

**These are next to MAX8734A chip 2 mosfets on left side this is good board**

**PQ39 mosfet 19.6v across one side all 4 legs**
**5.14 across the other side**

**Mosfet right beside it I could nor read the number**
**0v across the top side**
**5.14 across the bottom**

On the other side of the MAX8734a there are 2 more mosfet side by side
The first one
PU10 19v across the left side all 4 term
3.39 on all 4 right terminals

The mosfet right by it
First 3 term on left are 0 v and the 4th is .07v
the other 4 terminals are 3.39v

The above readings are the working board not turned on but plugged into ac charger

NO the board that will not power on

PQ39 19.6 across the top 4

1.9v across the bottom 4

The mosfet right below it 0v across the top 4

1.9 on first 3 and 1.6 on last

PU10
18.26 on the left side 4
.05 on the right side 4

The one beside it
0v on the 4 on left
.05 on the 4 on the right

DV6000 no power

Max8734A readings good board

Top side Left to right
0v 0v 0v 2.0v 0v 0v 2.0v 0v 0v 0v 5.0v 5.0v 0v 0v

Bottom side Left to right

5.13v 5.13v 1.36v 5.13v 0v 18v 5.16v 3.40v .07v 3.4v 3.39v 3.38v 8.03v

Board with no power

Top side left to right
1.6v 0v 0v 0v .19v 0v 0v 0v 0v .17v 1.89v 1.83v 0v 0v

Bottom side left to right

**1.65v 1.39v 1.68v 0v 1.66v .04v 0v 0v 0v 0v 0v 0v 0v 1.45v**

## Solution:

You can check the datasheet of max8734, 20 pin is VIN – should have 18V input, after you have 18V input the chip will output a 5V and send to pin 3 and 4 to switch on the chip to output 3.3V and 5V.

To solve the board with no power, first you have to make VIN to max8734. I don't think max8734 has problem in here, problem is in some other place.

## Problem:038

**I have a HP dv1000 which powers off suddenly. Sometimes it boots, sometimes turns off while booting and sometimes turns off while in POST. Same thing if powered just motherboard from my bench supply. Any idea about where to start?**

## Solution:

I have delt with this problem on these several times. as well as Compaq V2000 (they are the same motherboard.) 9 out of 10 x it is the CPU getting hot. sometimes I can clean the heat sink and CPU and add AS5 it is fine other times I have to replace the Fan. cleaned some liquid spills near EC and that fix the problem .

## Problem: 039

**Asus laptop: When i plug in the power, if i press the power button,you could hear the starting music of asus, but no display, even the faint image on the screen.**

## Solution:

It indicates vga problem. most asus notebooks are very strange, you can run and load windows without vga chip or vga card. You can try it, take off vga card and boot the machine and minutes later you can hear windows start up sound.

# Problem: 040

**I have a Toshiba A200 PSAF6A-02H01N which I am trying to replace the hard drive but it Appears to be overheating.**

## Solution:

Heat will not damage your hard disk. put in hdd, power up and see hdd start to spin or not. if it is not, then the problem is the power to hdd may have problem. but if it spin and you can't see it in bios, or it take long time to get into bios, it may have problem on south bridge or incorrect frequency from clock chip.

# Problem: 041

**mbx-165 with circuit protection problem**

## Solution:

when the PQ20 -PUMB2 is not solder in the mobo i get the correct voltage 9v at gate in PQ26

DC_IN_G1
Same as the motherboard, the pq26's G (DC_IN_G1) has 18V so DC_IN_R not present. DC_MOS_IN

is 18V, pq25's G is 9V. So charging chip max1909 should be fine.

First I check the AC_OFF_3#, which is very low, it should be high voltage.

To check if there is other problem of the motherboard (I bypass the AC_OFF_3# signal, a

short cut or lazy way to fix problem), I fly a wire between pr188 and pq23's third pin.

Now, the DC_IN_R has 18V, fine. but system standby power 3/5V is missing. touch the max8734

and find it very hot. Change it but still the same. i Use oscilloscope to monitor both pq64

and pq65's pin 1, no wave or pulse to find when plug in power so max8734 never start to

work. check max8734's 3 an 4 pin, find voltage is only 0.6v, something wrong here. This is a

signal call ALW_ON. Really hard to fix now, because ALW_ON involves too many components.

I decided to start from the simplest before moving up to EC or south bridge. Remove PD10,

still same problem. Remove PD24, standby power comes up. Measure PD24's 3 pin, only about 4

ohms so that is the reason, it pull ALW_ON low. Check schematic section of PU1 to PD24,

nothing important except control ALW_ON and AC_OFF_3#, so decide not to put pd24 back and

forget about rest. Try to power up and everything fine now.


## Problem: 042

Motherboard start and load windows but i can hear a ugly noise from the cpu socket zone, the
max8734 is new but maybe something damage the max8734. I test with oscilloscope and the wave in PQ65 is
a little different between Motherboard fail and working Motherboard .

## Solution:

It is the inductors dry joint.

# Problem: 043

**can i replace this mosfet with ALPHA & OMEGA ao4427**

## Solution:

yes, you can. every 8 pins mosfet has diode, what you saw maybe the ZD? don't worry about

that. You saw FDS6675BZ , but not all have a diode between GATE and SOURCE , I see the two

datasheet and the arrow of diode is in different direction .

# Problem: 044

**How do you know when you need 5v to open this mosfet? i need more info about how works the**

**mosfets and transistor? what value need to check in datasheet to know what voltage needed at**

**gate to open ?**

## Solution:

On most schematic voltage ratings are specified 5,4v needed to open gate, checked voltage

with battery charged attached and there is present 5,4v...without battery and only ac

attached there is 0v,all other voltage are present, missing only acok voltage, usually on mos

datasheet the g voltage is present (it's not a fixed voltage, is something between 3-12v

depending on type of mosfeet, on laptops usually it's 4-5 volts).

# Problem: 045

The eeprom is located in IC3201 , this is an ST microelectronic M24C08 W in TSSOP8 (DW) , i will try to read whit WILLEM PCB 5 PROGRAMMER , have you any idea about decode the dump bin file

## Solution:

Before any hardware work, if phoenix bios based try crysis recovery first.

# Problem: 046

I am having problem whit toshiba A300 , in inverter circuit , i try with 2 inverter and a new backlight and no luck

## Solution:

You should try and see if all voltage are presents at inverter input...once happened to me with an dv2000....about a few hrs of work found that the lid switch was faulty so inverter voltage missing to power on the lamp.

# Problem: 047

I have an ACER with mobo COMPAL LA-3581 , i see that i have about 15-17 volts in the POWER_SW button , not 3.3 usually , i think i need check the signal MAINPWON but im not sure , i see MAINPWON is in LM393 IC , can you tell if the MAINPWON is the signal of the power button? I remember in a HP probook i replaced LM393a whit LM393 and the power button have also 15v , after this is solder a lm393a and goto 3.3v , now i know that lm393 and lm393a are different.

## Solution:

Yes, for this mode of acer the power button should be about 17V.

Mainpwon and SHDN switch max8744 output on, so if you have 3ALW and 5ALW just don't worry about this signal.

The signal of Mainpwon is combined from VL (LDO of max8744) and PACIN. LDO of Max8744 will auto generate once Max8744 get power.

To switch off 3,5ALW output in battery mode (standby), it uses VS. VS comes from VIN. VIN is 0 when in battery mode. When you push the power button in battery mode(look at 51on# and pq4), VS will come from b+++ and then output 3,5VALW.

## Note:

I explain the usage of Mainpwon and VS. When you have

the power plug in, there should have high voltage in all 3 pins of pq4. B+ will be high,

because it is from VIN – actual B+ is the common point of external power and battery. VIN is

high. 51on# is high so the mos is in stop state.

If the power not plug in and battery present, VIN will be low and VS will be low too. VS low

will disable 3, 5VALW output, but to power up machine you need these 2 powers. 51ON# is the

signal to convert b+ into VS, when 51on# pull low the pq4 will convert B+ to VS therefore

Max8744 will output 3/5 valw.

## Problem: 048

**My Lenovo T60p has out of the blue started getting a single horizontal black line across the screen. I am thinking that the LCD cable has been damaged, but would like your opinion and suggestions before I consider doing anything.**

## Solution:

The laptop has a communication problem between battery and EC if there is message indicate no battery detected.

LCD cable should be ok, because one wire in lcd cable control much more than one line on LCD, so you will see much worse problem if there is even one wire has problem in the LCD cable. If you see something like snow interference on TV, that will be 100% LCD cable fault.

You should try a different LCD first.

# Problem:049

**Inspiron 2650 with a 8N816 mb (same mb as Inspiron 8600)**

**The front panel charging led and XP power meter show battery charging when AC adapter is first plugged in, but then it stops- battery never reaches more than 3%. The time before it stops varies- from a few minutes to 10 or more minutes.**

# Solution:

My suggestion is try different battery. Looks like the mb is ok, because if it was fault you wouldn't charge the battery from 0% to 3%.

# Problem: 050

**Hi, I have an ASUS F3SV out of warranty. The graphics card doesn't seem to function properly. I think it's an nVidia mobile gfx card with the TV tuner built in. If I enable the driver for it, I get screen corruption as soon as anything graphical happens. I can get it to work with basic functions by removing the driver and then using the standard vga driver, but this means I cant do anything with it. Can't even change the screen brightness and . Is this a problem with the gfx card, the main memory, or the driver? If it's hardware, is it easy to fix/repair/replace?**

## Solution:

Hi, this is fault design of NV chips. You can't do anything, need to replace with new chip (made after 09). The cost to change chip is not so cheap, the chip cost more than $45, plus labor you look at around $280. Make sure at least you get 6 month warranty and get chip replaced. Because by just reheating the old chip it can run about 2 month then fail again. I know some computer shops offer cheap price to just reflow solders and not change chip, they only give 1 to 3 month warranty. I don't think it is a proper way to fix laptop and in the most case is a cheating to the customers. Every time when I encounter NV chip problem, I request my customers to replace chips – even risker than just reflow and more expensive than just reflow, otherwise I wouldn't fix it.

## Problem: 051

I have problem with acer 5920 mobo ZD1 , the lcd screen dont turn on , i have another 5920 working i see a problem in U1 AAT4280 page 18 , when ac adaptor is present in fail mobo have about 1v in pin1 (OUT) but in the working mobo only have 0.30v , y check the diodes in signal LCDVCC and are ok R10 is good also , and measuring resistance to gnd in pin1 in working mobo is about 1M ohm and in fail mobo only give me a value if put tester in 200M ohm scale , and the resistance start in 1-2M ohm and go up.
I will try to replace AAT4280 in a few days , what you think?

## Solution:

U1 has 1 input- on/off, 1 output – lcdvcc and 1 vin – +3V. The input are int_lvds_digon and ev_lvds_vdden, the first one is for the motherboards that use intel integrated video and second is for the motherboards that use mxm plug in video card. Only one of two can have high voltage at a time, can't be both high at same time.

In the normal working motherboard, the pin 6 should be 3V, the pin 3 should be but most be the 3V. pin 1 should be 3V it is the power source for LCD.

If the pin 3 is low when you switch on the machine, the problem is either vga card or north bridge.

In your situation, you don't need to check the resistance to the gnd unless you suspect u1 has been burnt. And also it has nothing to do with power supply.

the 3 things you need to check after machine power up:

1. pin 6 has 3V?
2. pin 3 has 3V?
3. pin 1 has 3V and LCD connector CN1's pin 3 and 5 has 3V?

## Question:

**Does Ec mean Electrical circuit?**

## Anwser:

**EC has other names such as SIO, Keyboard Controller.**

## Problem: 052

**Hi i replace the U1 but still not work , pin3= 0v**
**I replaced the MXM graphic card and the LCD on again , pin3= 3v , the fail is graphic card .**

## Solution:

Next time, don't worry to replace U1, unless you have all other voltage but not the pin 1.

Because pin 3 is the condition and pin 1 is the result. If the condition is fault where will

the result comes from?

To be a good repairer, average time to spend on one machine can't not be longer than 1 hour.

I have average time of 1.5 hour, still not fast enough.

# Problem: 053

**I need some advice on a HP DV2000 verve laptop.**

**I bought it 3 years ago and I've had several issues with it. I had to replace the HDD after**

**1 year (1 week after it came out of warranty). In March last year, the graphics chip died**

**and I had it replaced for $350. The graphics died again 2 months ago and that was the last**

**straw and I went and bought a new Dell XPS.**

# Solution:

Your dv2000 probably had a NVidia 8400M GPU. These had a manufacturing fault that meant they

would die at some point. From what I can tell, it would happen when they got a little to

hot. The one I had died when the laptop was 18 months old and it was the first time a 3D

game was played on it. There isn't really anything you can do about this. The only

replacement GPU you can use have the same problem. So buying a new motherboard the won't fix

it. There are people selling reconditioned motherboards and most will include a copper

insert to fill the gap between the GPU and the heat sink. This should help keep the GPU cool

but it is still a time bomb.

With mine I have done two things. The first was to pull it apart and reflow the solder on the GPU (google that to find what I mean). This got it working but was only temporary. Some people seem to claim it is a long term fix. Late last year I bought a second hand motherboard from one of the older versions of the laptop. This has a Nvidia 7200 GPU on it. But, I forgot about the CPU. When I installed the motherboard with the original CPU, it didn't boot. I happened to have a CPU from another machine and it worked. That CPU is a Core Solo T1300 and is painfully slow. I've order a CPU that should work and am waiting for that to arrive. And a new power switch as I pulled the wires off. In the end I'll have a working laptop, but it probably isn't going to be worth the money I have spent.

This is design problem of NV graphic chip, only can solve the problem by replacing NV chip made after 37th week of 2009. The new chip should be easily last more than one year(I mean 95% of them). In Melbourne, my shop is the only place replacing with new NV chip (my dealers or other computer shops I do the repair jobs for them also had the chip replaced). If you are in Melbourne, I can repair it for you for free as long as this machined has been repaired by me and also not over 12 month yet.
$350 is too much, I charge people $280 in my shop and offer 6 month warranty.

There isn't really anything you can do about this. The only replacement GPU you can use have the same problem.
Nvidia issued the redesigned chips on 37th week of 2009, said overcame the problem. But as we know, 2 mode of G86 chip, the one with mark G86-631-A2 has no problem at all, the one with mark G86-630-A2 still has certain faulty rate. The reason is G86-631-A2 has build-in temperature controller and the other one does not have.
Go7200 chip still have the same problem as G86, for those made before 37th week of 09. The replacement should be the one made after that date and has T mark, Go7200T.

I think I explained the issue in previous post, the reason why it happened and what kind of design fault of it, why use the hot air to reflow it can temporary solve the problem.

The motherboard you bought and try to use on your DV2000 machine, not only has different CPU, but also has different touchpad. G86 (8400M) has 4 wire connector and Go7200 has 7 wire connector, you may need to change touchpad as well.

# Problem: 054

Now i have a satellite A100 , mobo INVENTEC SAN ANTONIO , the ac adaptor is 15v i test and the Q519 is closed , have 15v at gate and 15v at source , but no power on +VBAT , the charger is BQ24721 , VCC is good 15v at R619 but ACDET is only 1.3v and VREF5 is in 0 volt , you think BQ24721 is fail , or you can tell me other test before remove the BQ24271 ?

## Solution:

BQ24721 fails a lot, I usually change 24721 first.

# Problem: 055

I have dv9000 QUANTA AT7 , not found AT7 schematic but AT6 match all , have voltje 19v fine , also 3v and 5v present (max8734) and the power button have 3.3v , but when press power the mobo don't do nothing , no leds no fan , etc ... i have also an AT3 working , i see in 1.5v AT3 use MAX8717 and when AC adaptor is plug have 5v at DL1 and DL2 for gates PQ38 PQ35. Then i go to AT7 and check DL1 DL2 for MAX8743 at gates PQ33 PQ28 , and only see 0 volt , maybe i will try first to remove this 2 mosfet and check again ? this 2 mosfet dont seem short maybe the MAX8743 is fail , what is your advice about this ?

## Solution:

First, there is nothing to do with pq28, pq33, those are for 1.5V output.

Second, check the EC working conditions when the machine can't fire up. In those DV9000, pay

more attention on LID_EC#, this signal must be 3.3 before machine can fire up. If this one is

low, try to get 3.3V from somewhere to it.

# Problem: 056

**I have a Quanta AT3 (dv6700) that will not power on. I have the AT3 schematic and a mid to**

**low end multimeter. At this point I know about 30% of what would be required to effectively**

**interpret the schematic. So I'm a little ill-equipped, but I'm learning.**

**What I've determined so far is that the DCIN voltage (PIN 1) on the MAX8724 chip is reading**

**low at 0.13v. What I'm not sure about is where to go from here. It seems that PQ40 may be a**

**suspect but I'm not sure how to test.**

## Solution:

The 8724 is a battery charging chip, also is part of protection circuit. 8724 malfunction

may affect PRWSRC, which is the whole system power.

DCIN of 8724 comes from VAD-1, you need to check PD17 first, then PD16. Common problem of

this mobo, Both pd17 and pd16 easy to be burnt.

I assume #1 is PD16. Is #2 PD17? Both are obviously toasted. Also, just out of curiosity, is

#3 PQ40? There are a lot of components in that area with no labels so I'm a little unsure.

# Problem: 057

**HP 550 laptop.**

**I recently changed to a new charger works fine. But when i move it in a certain way it stops charging. I'm pretty sure its the laptop that is the problem.**

## Solution:

Change the charging unit on the motherboard

# Problem: 058

**i found test point T161 to check the LID_EC# , and 3v is not present**

## Solution:

Capacitors on the graphic card are not so easy to fail, it only has about 5 ohm when you

Measure it, it is normal because internal resistance of graphic card just like that.

Once you find LID_EC# is low, you simply connect a power to it, let's say the 3V power for

EC, connect a 10k resistor from 3V to LID_EC# pin. The purpose of LID_EC is let EC knows if

the lid is closed or not, once it is low the EC thinks the LID is closed and refuse to send

PWRBTN signal to south bridge, the PWRBTN is the signal invoke machine withdraw from S5

state and enter into S3 state, or people say switch on machine (actually, switch on machine

is pull up RSMRST – but RSMRST in most case is high, only after you remove the cmos battery

then it becomes low. So, when RSMRST is high and mobo wait for PWRBTN signal to become live

– this state we call it S5.)

# Problem: 059

These capacitors are really burn in 0 Ohms , i replaced these 2 capacitors and now at TEST

POINT T161 have about 1v but still not trying to power , also i try put 3.3 at LID with a

external power supply and no way , the only see at the moment is DL1 and DL2 dont have 5v in

MAX8743 .

## Solution:

"Capacitors on the graphic card are not so easy to fail, it only has about 5 ohm when you

Measure it, it is normal because internal resistance of graphic card just like that."

# Problem: 060

I have a Asus f3jp thats 166ghz core2duo processor, 2 gigs of RAM (i think), and 250mb
Radeon x1700 video card. I am currently running windows 7.
I've found that previously Football Manager 2009 would run on my computer fine, but lately
the laptop is overheating and then shutting down very quickly after starting up a game like
this or minecraft. However when running general windows and non-graphical applications (eg. browsing),
overheating isn't an issue. I opened up a few panels off the back of the laptop to see if its a dust issue, but i
couldn't find any (that said I didn't get very deep inside).

Any idea what could be wrong and is it worth fixing?

## Solution:

The ASUS F3 Series laptops have a single large access panel on the bottom, so I don't

understand how you can open "a few panels". When you open this panel, the heatsink with the

fan in it should be right in front of you. Pull the fan out and look inside the heatsink. It

will probably be filled with dust on the exhaust vent side.

If that doesn't help, pull the heatsink off. It is actually two parts. One has the fan and

covers the GPU. The other is the actual outlet vents with a heatpipe going to the CPU. Pull

both off, clean them and the contacts with the CPU and GPU. Then apply thermal compound to

the CPU and GPU and put the heatsinks back on.

You can also consider undervolting the CPU. The first few posts of

http://forum.notebookreview.com/showthread.php?t=235824 explain how to do this. For my old

F3Sv, it was good for about 5ºC at idle and over 10ºC when stressed. With the fan/vent

cleaning, the overall effect was something like 10ºC at idle and about 20ºC when stressed.

# Problem: 061

**Dell Inspiron 9400 aka E1705.**
**When i power it on all what i see is the power LED "green" turns on for 3 sec.**
**i tried everything, stripping all the drives and now i am down to only keyboard and one ram and still same issue. tried it with bat and ac adapter**

## Solution:

Take off the vga card and power computer, see if it still shut off.

# Problem: 062

**The circuit comprising PU11 (a TI TL331 single comparator), PQ62, PC195 and PD20 form a**

**charge pump circuit to provide a boosted +ve gate drive [VH28] to PQ61 (a large N-channel**

**MOSFET – top left of the schematic).**

**The circuit comprising PU11 (a TI TL331 single comparator), PQ62, PC195 and PD20 form a**

**charge pump circuit to provide a boosted +ve gate drive [VH28] to PQ61 (a large N-channel**

**MOSFET – top left of the schematic).**

**Without this gate drive, no DC input from the power adapter can be fed into the laptop.**

**Hence the sometimes flashing battery LED when the power button is pressed. There is enough**

**juice to power the system controller, but no feed to the charger.**

## Solution:

i agree with you, such design is not only unnecessary but also worse than bad. what we did to

overcome this problem is replace pq61 with a diode, replace pq3 with another diode, of

course the condition to do this is battery charging part work alright.

# Problem: 064

**i have Toshiba satellite P200-1JV laptop. It runs on battery without any problem.**
**it does not run with a/c. does not charge battery.**

**when i plug in a/c without battery the a/c light on laptop blinks. press the power**
**button and nothing happens.**

**put battery in laptop with a/c power on, a/c light on laptop stops blinking and**
**battery charge light comes on but does not charge battery. press power button**
**and laptop will run until battery is exhausted.**

**the a/c charger is new and correct spec for laptop.**

**any advice on how to diagnose fault, like what area to check, mosfet, chips etc**

## Solution:

first check all mobo marks to found mobo model and if you can found the schematic , then you

need to found one mosfet 8 pin sop8 that is connected directly to DC JACK , and then found

the next mosfet connected whit the first mosfet , when you conect AC you need this 2 mosfet

open , 19volts at DRAIN SOURCE , and about 8-10volts at GATE to open , usually is controlled

by the IC charger circuit , maybe have a short in AC circuit side or IC charger not

recognize the adapter and no open mosfets .

# Problem: 065

i have managed to obtain schematic for Toshiba P200.there are two different sets of mosfets

controlled by two different charging ic.i like to confirm with you which one to test

## Solution:

if you  check all you motherboard to confirm it is LA-3711P , then you need to start to

check PQ8 PQ9 , look for short after PQ8 between PQ8 PQ9 , if work fine with battery no short

on P3 B+ . then you need to have 19v at source drain in both mosfet and 8-10v at gate of

both PQ8 PQ9 pin4 , ACON PACIN control this gates , if you have 19v at pin4 PQ8 PQ9 the

mosfets are closed and then you don't have the 19v at PQ9 pin5,6,7,8 that you need for laptop

to work with AC adapter.

# Problem:  066

i have tested PQ8 and PQ9.results are as follows.
PQ8 is AO4407. pin 1,2,3 is 19.37v. pin 5,6,7,8 is 19.36v. pin 4
gate is 19.37v.

PQ9 is AO4407. pin 1,2,3 is 19.37v. pin 5,6,7,8 is 11-12.00v.
pin 4 is 19.37v.

i have set meter on diode mode and put positive on pin 2-3 and
negative on 6-7 the meter beeps and shows resistance of 0.6 ohms, then i reversed the

positive – negative ,meter beeps again
shows resistance of 0.6.it beeps both ways. this is PQ8.

i have done same as above with PQ9 and it shows resistance of
25kohm both ways.

could short on PQ8 make gate voltage high on both mosfets?
what do i need to check to find out why voltage is 19.36v.at gate

## Solution:

GATE PQ8 PQ9 are connected between, are in the same line (trace), if PQ8 is burn please

check also PQ19 , another ao4407 are connected in the same DRAIN SOURCE , you need to remove

from motherboard and test in continuity or 200 Ohms scale , if you see 0 – 10 Ohms between

drain source it is burnt for sure , check then PQ19 .
You need 19v at PQ9 pin 5,6,7,8 but if PQ8 is burnt it will not work . PU4 ISL6251 is the

charger IC.


XXXXXXXXXXXXXXXXXXXXXXXXXXXXXXXXXXXXXXXXXXXXXXXXXXXXXXXXXXXXXXXXXXXXXXXXX

## Problem: 067

**Component Level Motherboard Repair (Not replacement)**

**How do you diagnose the exact component failure?**

## Solution:

Obviously, a burn mark is a dead give away, but what if there are no visual signs? Do you

poke around with a multi-meter? With what voltage settings and how do you know what to look

for?

## Problem: 068

**Is it usually a bad capacitor?**
**badcaps seems to think so. What about a bad connection?<p>**

**How do you perform the component level repair?**

**So you've found the bad capacitor or component, can you really solder a new one on without hurting the components around them? What's a good soldering iron for under $100?<p>**

# Solution:

**Diagnose problem:**

This is the hardest part in notebook repair. Basically, we measure voltages on motherboard and there are few power supply range from 1V to 12V on the motherboard. For example, north bridge needs 1.05V, 1.2V, 1.5V, 1.8V, 2.5V, depends on model of north bridge.<p>

We also measure all sort of signals, such as PCIRST, CPURST, CLK. We measure the resistances of each AD line from north bridge to CPU/RAM.<p>

We watch the current changing patterns to get rough idea where is the problem

There are some simple steps to follow when checking a notebook motherboard:

1. make sure main system powers are ready, that is 3V and 5V.
2. switching circuit is ok, which involves IO/Keyboard controller, south bridge
3. power sequence is ok, which you can see the current jump up and down for few times.
4. all the necessary signals are not missing.

**About Bad Cap:**

It happens but only about 10% in those motherboards need to repair, and it is the easiest fault to repair no matter if the cap was burnt or not.<br>

**Loose connection:**

Mostly happen on VGA chips, south bridges and the places close to CPU. Hard to troubleshoot and need lot experiences.

**How to repair?:**

You need specialized tools. I have DC power supply which can display current change and set to different voltage and current output. You need Really nice soldering station, SMD rework station, BGA rework station, etc. I also have more than thousand schematic diagrams, all together about 10GB and you could not find anywhere in the net.<p>

I have seen the video in youTub teach people how to fix VGA problem, and I guess you only have 30% chance if you follow it. My BGA rework station tutorial can perform up to 95% successful rate.

XXXXXXXXXXXXXXXXXXXXXXXXXXXXXXXXXXXXXXXXXXXXXXXXXXXXXXXXXXXXXXXXXXXXXXXXXXXXXXXX

# Problem:  069

**Troubleshooting Dead HP G6000 Motherboard**

**Things that are likely worth solving:**

**Bad capacitors. Decently common and the parts only cost a few cents.**
**Most of the ICs on board... 4-20 pin jobbies such as the power ic do fail and are swappable**

**for less than a buck or so**

**Blown fuses. Easy to diagnose easy to replace. This is a definite.**

**Any and all damaged jacks. Power and audio being the most commonly broken.**

**Resistors. easy to find easy to replace. cost is in pennies.**

**Transistors and diodes can be more problematic to diagnose and fix but they too are cheap**

**and swappable with just a soldering iron.**

**Obviously you can swap cpus so you should be able to diagnose that as well.**

## Solution:

*Case Study 1*

"Machine: HP G6000(same mainboard as V6000)
Problem: Laptop will not power up, completely dead

Description: The machine has been water damaged. It does not have system standby power, which are 3V and 5V.

Finding The Fault:

Check Max8724(the battery charging chip) first, because to make system has standby power this chip must work correctly. This is a 28 pin chip, we only need to test 1, 2, 4, 8, 10, 11 pin. They are VIN(main power for chip), LDO(provide 3.3V for chip itself in order to set REF voltage, also provide signal to drive 2 MOS to charge battery), REF(set reference voltage of the chip), SHDN#(enable/disable chip, a switch), ACIN(indicate the power supply has plugged in), ACOK#(power adaptor ok with mainboard).

Everything ok except 10 pin, ACIN is 0V. This is incorrect, mainboard doesn't detect there is an adaptor! Trace it backward and find it is very simple – mainboard use 2 resistors to pull the input voltage(19V, directly from dc socket) down to about 4V, so test the first resistor and find it opened. Change it and 3V/5V power come up and mainboard be able to switch on.

Then the trouble start when I try to charge the battery. The charging current never go beyond 0.15A and after 10 seconds the charging light start to flashing. Also can't switch on from battery. First, change Max8724, still same problem. Next check all the resistors around max8724 and change it if it has any sign of watering, still no good. Then change KB3926(EC/KBC, chip monitors the statue of battery), still same.

Decide to check MBDATA and MBCLCK, 2 signals that send battery information from battery to KB3926 before I give up. I find the MBDATA is short!

Finally, find there are 2 pins stick together on CN10(the connector of multimedia switch board). Fix it and it start to charging battery. Switch on with power adaptor, ok. Remove the power adaptor once switch on, battery keep the mainboard running, ok. But still can't

switch on from battery once remove the power adaptor. Think, think, do I miss something here

or there? Oh, the CMOS battery not installed, put the CMOS battery back and everything work

perfectly. The battery part of troubleshooting takes me about 3 hours.

Remember, system may not run if you don't have CMOS battery or CMOS battery is low for some

AMD cpu mainboard.

# Problem: 070

*Case Study 2*

**"Machine: Acer 4600**
**Problem: Laptop will not power up**

**Description: The machine wont turn on when customer bring in.**

# Solution:

1. plug in our power supply and it shows short circuit on board, the current jump to the 5A,

which is the limit of my power supply.
2. take off the mobo, drop the voltge of power supply to 5v, limit current to about 1A, plug

in again and find a mos very hot.
3. replace this mos, now the short circuit fixed.
4. turn on, the current goes up to 0.3A and stopped, it should go up to 1A during booting.

5. touch cpu, not hot, no power to cpu.
6. check the cpu pwm, which is max1907a. all conditions to make it work are present, but

still no power output. the ref voltege is 0. so most likely this chip gone.
7. I replace the chip and everything work fine.

# Problem: 071

**Dell inspiron 6400 with a power problem.**

**Laptop can't run nor charge the battery on adapter, but on battery it run.**

## Solution:

This is typical protection circuit problem. check the 2 mosfet just after power socket

# Problem: 07x

**Charging problem**

**C700's charging chip is 39A126, DV6000/9000's charging chip is max8724 or max8725. Check the**

**working conditions of those chips. such as VIN, ACIN, ACOK, LDO, REF, SHDN.<p>**

## Solution:

Charging problem is second hardest problem on notebook repairing, the first one is signal

level – everything looks ok but just no display.

# Problem: 072

**usb no power**

## Solution:

The following solution only apply that usb has no power, if the usb device get power but

can't be detected or can't be recognized by system, that indicates south bridge problem.
To get power for usb is very simple. use multimeter to find out which usb pin is ground, the

pin on the other side will be the power. for example say pin 4 is ground so pin 1 will be

the power.

connect power pin to 5v you can find on motherboard, usually a big inductor(be careful, when you measure the voltage, put battery in as well, some mobo the inductor for charging circuit give you 5v if you don't put battery in but jump to battery voltage once you put in the battery, such high voltage will burn your usb devices). connect it on the different side of inductor that mosfet connect to(or should I say power out side?) so you can get smooth waveform, don't connect to the same side of mosfet(this is power in side).

# Problem: 073

**Dark image on the screen , just very hard to see, a torch will show it is there though).**

## Solution:

When we fix such problem, usually we do the following:

1. find an known good lamp or screen, plug into inverter see if its light up. if it lights

up so you need to change your screen's lump.
2. if it not light up, do following:
a. check power(either 5V or 19V), enable signal(3V), brightness control(3V) are presented.

(all testing by done with adaptor plug in).
b. if all those presented, then change inverter otherwise
c. need to find out which wire is power, which is enable, which is brightness people find

hard in here because they don't know how to find out which is which.

Power always connect to fuse (also need to check fuse is ok). for the other two, you need to check inverter pwm's datasheet to make decision. Just start from pwm's EN and Brightness pin, trace back to connector. After you find out, make sure all these wires has normal resistance to ground, otherwise you have to cut off the wire that abnormal. Then try to find exact voltage from mobo and connect to inverter, by doing this you are not really fix the problem but bypass it. It is a easy to work around it rather than fix problem.

# Problem: 074

**The first step to troubleshooting is monitor the current change. usually, current reading can tell what was wrong and quite accurate.**

**You frequently mention monitoring the current change to pinpoint the area of failure. Can you please describe this troubleshooting technique in more detail with some guidelines and numbers to look for?**

## Solution:

To understand why current changing, you may need to know the basic powering states of notebook – which is called ACPI standard – S0 to S5.

S0 is full running state, S5 is state that after you switch off laptop but with either power or battery presented. out off topic here, the S5 is the state after you shut down computer not the state you just plug in the power. Power button is for wake up computer from S5 and enter into S3. In ACPI standard, to switch on computers you need a signal "RSMRST". It explains why some laptops auto switch on if there is no CMOS battery, because its EC send RSMRST when power plug in. But you need push power button to switch on laptop if there is CMOS battery, because laptop remembers it is in S5 state.

Powering up a laptop can be divided into few parts, first check south bridge's gpio definition, check communication between bios and south bridge, check system ram, power cpu, power up vga. so you can see the current goes up and down. step by step it reaches to full power.

Current changing monitor is just give you rough idea, sometimes not so accurate.
let's see 2 examples:

1. a hp 530, power up but stay on 0.68A. it should go down a bit after 0.68A, and up again.

The faulty mobo current change is 0.02 – 0.3 -0.68. After we see this current, we know it

may have problem on SB or may be on NB but most likely is SB.

I check LPC 0 to LPC 3, no signal find. it may have problem on SB or BIOS. So I flash the

BIOS before I do anything on SB. It was fixed after I reflash BIOS.

2. DV9000. Normal mobo: 0.01 – 0.3 -0.9 – 1.1 – 0.9 – 1.2 -1.45 then display.
we find faulty mobo 0.01-0.3-0.9-1.1-0.9, by checking DMI Link we find there is one or two

pulses. So we have an idea that it already pass memory checking, the next stage is VGA

checking and active VGA output. In here, if it stop in 1.1 it most likely NB or SB problem,

but if it stop in 0.9 or after, it may be the problem of VGA.

Current changing gives you an idea about where is the fault but not 100% accurate. People

ask me what fault by just give me the current reading and I always say you need to give me

the changing states, how many jumps that current made.


XXXXXXXXXXXXXXXXXXXXXXXXXXXXXXXXXXXXXXXXXXXXXXXXXXXXXXXXXXXXXXXXXXXXXXXXXXXXXX

# Problem: 075

**How to diagnose motherboards on a component level. What tools needed?**

## Solution:

I find it is very hard to explain this. actually, it is very simple and can be described in

two words: current and signal. read the current change during booting tells you where the

machine stopped. check the signals on the different part of motherboard tells what is wrong

or what is  missing.

Tools are: smd rework station, bga rework station, power supply has current meter. all the

rest tools you can find in any radio tv repair shop, of course all the datasheets for the

components, especially the schematic diagram, you will find it much difficult without it.

# Problem: 076

could short on PQ8 make gate voltage high on both mosfets?
what do i need to check to find out why voltage is 19.36v.at gate

i have tested PQ8 and PQ9.results are as follows.
PQ8 is AO4407. pin 1,2,3 is 19.37v. pin 5,6,7,8 is 19.36v. pin 4
gate is 19.37v.

PQ9 is AO4407. pin 1,2,3 is 19.37v. pin 5,6,7,8 is 11-12.00v.
pin 4 is 19.37v.

i have set meter on diode mode and put positive on pin 2-3 and
negative on 6-7 the meter beeps and shows resistance of 0.6 ohms,then i reversed the

positive – negative ,meter beeps again shows resistance of 0.6.it beeps both ways. this is

PQ8. i have done same as above with PQ9 and it shows resistance of
25kohm both ways.

## Solution:

 GATE PQ8 PQ9 Should be connected  in the same line (trace) , if PQ8 is burn please check

also PQ19 , another ao4407 are connected in the same DRAIN SOURCE , you need to remove from

mobo and test in continuity or 200 Ohms scale , if you see 0 – 10 Ohms between drain source

is burn sure , check then PQ19 .

You need 19v at PQ9 pin 5,6,7,8 but if PQ8 is burn not work . PU4 ISL6251 is the charger IC.

# Problem: 077

Toshiba satellite P200-1JV laptop. It runs on battery without any problem.
it does not run with a/c. does not charge battery.

## Solution:

first check all mobo marks to found mobo model and if you can found the schematic , then you need to found one mosfet 8 pin sop8 that is connected directly to DC JACK , and then found

the next mosfet connected with the first mosfet , when you connect AC you need this 2 mosfet

open , 19volts at DRAIN SOURCE , and about 8-10volts at GATE to open , usually is controlled

by the IC charger circuit , maybe have a short in AC circuit side or IC charger not

recognize the adapter and no open mosfets

# Problem: 078

**Having problems whit dell xps M1530**

**Don't do nothing when press power button , ACAV_IN is present at Q5 Q6 (3.2V) i have**

**DCBATOUT but 3v and 5v not present , i  check DCBATOUT for U69 TPS51120 and is OK , then**

**check VREG3 VREG5 and also work fine , but i don't have 3V/5V_EN to activate outputs , Q17 is**

**not in mobo only pads , D16 have 0.06v at 3V/5V_EN and 3.3v at PURE_HW_SHUTDOWN# , maybe**

**need S5_ENABLE to activate 3v and 5v ? what you think about the next step to check ? maybe**

**some signals in KBC WPC8763L .**

## Solution:

At the moment the TPS51120 is working , use power supply  to put 2.5V in D16 3V/5V_EN and

the 3V 5V outputs go enable . find why S5_ENABLE and 3V/5V_EN are low .

# Problem: 079

**My D505 may power on boot OK or may have following condition.</h4>**
**a)LED flash**
**b)"da.da.da....." sound.**

## Solution:

 If you know the bios manufacturer, the beep code will tell you where the failure is.

So the number of beeps and the duration of each beep is a specific code from the bios to let you know what it couldn't start – like video, memory, cpu etc.

The north bridge dry joint, it is common fault of this model. BGA reworking on north bridge, and replace the north bridge if bga reworking doesn't work

# Problem:  080

It's a Toshiba Satellite A205-SP4077, Core 2 Duo. While replacing cracked LCD tried several panels with no success. <br>Then noticed LVDS RX2- signal from motherboard is missing.

## Solution:

 The north bridge dry joint, it is common fault of this model. BGA reworking on north bridge, and replace the north bridge if bga reworking doesn't work.

# Problem:  081

Dual screen problems

## Solution:

First, I don't think it is a good idea to use dual screens on laptop, you put extra loading onto the vga chip.

Second, the external monitor flicking means vga card try to setup the display mode and resolution on the monitor. It will be stable once it set the display mode and resolution.

# Problem:  082

I have a Gateway P-6825 Laptop that has no backlight on LCD. I have bought 2 inverters 2

LCD cables I have tons of screens no matter what I get no backlight.
It works perfect on external monitor and you can see it come on the LCD but the screen will

not light up. Also what is the normal input power to the inverter as well.

## Solution:

Inverter board input power sometimes is Vin or B+, close to AC adapter voltage. You may

check if is there a fuse in the LCD connector path. I'd suggest you search for the inverter

IC datasheet. For inverters using OZ960 there is an input called ENA which must be 3.3V for

enable inverter and another called DIM which is 3V for full brightness.

# Problem: 083

I have a Toshiba Satellite Pro A300, just tried to use the dvd rom and it's not working, it

won't acknowledge any dvd's, It won't even open, last time I used the dvd rom several months

ago everything worked fine and the notebook has not been moved

## Solution:

If the dvd drive it's ok (u should test it in another laptop), it's for sure a chipset

problem (the chip that controls the drive also, it's the intel ICH8M the U33A on the

schematic/board).I will exclude a connection port problem if the laptop hasn't fallen or

something like that. If drive is ok, try a reflow of that chip, should solve your problem.

# Problem: 084

Is a Toshiba Satellite L355-D-S7901, motherboard 6050A2175001-MB-A02, after POST starts to

beep continuously like a stuck key. I've tried even with bare motherboard (no keyboard

connected). Will appreciate any idea.

## Solution:

check capacitors that keyboard connected, or check keyboard controller.

# Problem: 085

**How to check Sony protection circuits**

**SONY VGN-NS11S MBX-195 M790 Rev 1.1 1P-0087J04-8011**

**PCG-7141M ,**

## Solution:

Sony's protection circuits are hard to troubleshoot. It is involved too many components. About mbx-165 protection circuits:

1. Power pass PF1 becomes DC_IN, at this point, Max1909 start to work. ACIN, DCIN high, LDO

5V, REF 2V(must have, can't remember exactly voltage). Max1909_PDS low to drive PQ25 (don't

know exactly voltage, but lower than DC_IN).

2. PQ25 convert DC_IN to DC_IN_MOS. Here comes the hardest to troubleshoot of sony

protection circuit.

PQ26's gate must be low and it was a signal call DC_IN_G1. So where this DC_IN_G1 from? In

normal situation, it max1909_pds through a resistor.
Now, you have 19V of this signal that is abnormal.

we check it by few steps:

1. check pc3, is it short?
2. ac_off_3# is high? if it is high, check check PQ31, PQ20, PR116, PR119, PR120.
3. ac_off_3# is low? check the ac_off_3# signal, many components involved: DC_IN part from

PD2 to AC_OFF_3#. From input of PU13 (2nd pin, max1909_LDO) to PQ24A, PQ59, PQ24B.

I hate sony's protection circuit, too many troubles. Last time I fix one of such problem on sony mobo is PD2 leaking, spend me almost 5-6 hours. And solution of it? Just remove the PD2, which means it does not matter if there is PD2 or not the mobo still, working. Extra Protection means extra troubles and faults.

# Problem: 086

**My Lenovo SL400 screen went dark (image there, just very hard to see, a torch will show it is there though).**

## Solution:

When we fix such problem, usually we do the following:

1. find an known good lamp or screen, plug into inverter see if its light up. if it lights

up so you need to change your screen's lamp.
2. if it not light up, do following:
a. check power(either 5V or 19V), enable signal(3V), brightness control(3V) are presented.

(all testing be done with adapter plug in).
b. if all those presented, then change inverter otherwise
c. need to find out which wire is power, which is enable, which is brightness.
people find hard in here because they don't know how to find out which is which.

Power always connect to fuse (also need to check fuse is ok). for the other two, you need to check inverter pwm's datasheet to make decision. Just start from pwm's EN and Brightness pin, trace back to connector. After you find out, make sure all these wires has normal resistance to ground, otherwise you have to cut off the wire that abnormal. Then try to find exact voltage from mobo and connect to inverter, by doing this you are not really fix the problem but bypass it. It is a easy to work around it rather than fix problem.

# Problem: 087

**1. Is there a popular model of power supply that you can recommend?**

**2. Do you use mini-grabbers to attach power supply to laptop or do you have a collection of common dc plugs?**

**3. How do you use with Dell laptops that have a third wire to identify the power supply?**

## Solution:

I just burn one power supply today, this is 4th one I have burnt in last 3 years. Lucky it was not connected to any laptop when it was burnt. It's output voltage was jump from 19V to 50V, at this voltage all laptop's power circuits will burn through, I have 3 laptops burnt before.

There is no popular model as I know, but at least 5A/30V. Get a industrial grade if it possible, because non-industrial grade power supply can't even run a laptop for more than one hour, or you face the risk to burn your power supply – in turn it will burn the laptop.

It is sufficient for repairing job but not enough for machine testing. It must have MA reading, because sometimes the reading is less than 0.01A.

I have all the collection of DC plugs, made from faulty chargers.

Ignore the 3rd pin of dell charger, it is only for PS_ID, only use for charging battery. Without this PS_ID machine still run but just can't charge. But some old dell like 5150 will not work our power supply, lucky we don't have any such machines to fix.

## Problem:  088

**1. Is there a "generic" current profile for laptops or does each laptop have it's own unique current profile?**

**2. In your example for DV9000, you say "0.01 – 0.3 -0.9 – 1.1 – 0.9 – 1.2 -1.45 then**

display" Can you explain what happens at each current change state?

3. Do you need a power supply that logs the current or does it change slow enough to visually monitor the different current states?

4. If a laptop gets power but no video, how do you isolate the failure between northbridge, southbridge, SIO, bios?

# Solution:

1. Every laptop has its unique current profile. But although the reading is different, the up and down (jumping) are similar.

2. The dv9000's current reading may not very accurate; I suggest you first move the ram away and see how the current changing, then put back the ram and check it again.

3. not very fast, your eyes can catch the changes.

4. this is a big question, may need a full text book to explain it. The simple answer for this question: a. current reading, b. LPC wave, c.SMB wave. we have explain the current reading before. LPC waves are measured on EC, if you can't find LPC wave, that means no communication between EC and SB, PLTRST present or not, if is not then SB problem, etc. SMB waves are measured on ram slot, communication between ram and northbridge, H_RESET present or not, if it is not then NB. There are also so many signals need to check.

I think the hardest fault for beginner is why the laptop not power up, not the faults after it powers up.

*lets see the example how we troubleshoot a non-powering machine,:*

Model: Acer  5737

EC: kbc926

symptom:  can't power up

checked: 3ALW, 5ALW presented

1. check the power button has power or not, press it to see if pull down the voltage.<p>
2. check kbc926's 32 pin, which is on/off see the signal received.
3. EC_VCCA is high?
4. check EC_RSMRST is high?
5. LID_SW# is high?
6. ACIN is high?
7. EC_CRY is correct?(32.76Khz)
8. South bridge crystal correct( which is X4, also 32.76KHz)
9. PBTN_OUT pull low when you press power button?

if all above have no problem, consider the south bridge fault. for this machine, there is a

single bridge – south bridge/north bridge/vga combined. North bridge's functions are mostly taken over by CPU.

# Problem: 089

**I am having problem switching on my dv9000 machine**

## Solution:

It is handy if you have a multimeter.

The power switch from DV9000 is same as DV6000. There is other way to switch on your machine and you will know if is ribbon cable problem or m/b problem.

The switches of most laptop ( include dv6000) are just pull a voltage to the ground and send a signal to EC (most people call it keyboard controller). So check your ribbon cable connector on the motherboard, on the 3rd pin( can't remember from left or right, but it doesn't matter you can try both) it should have 3.3V, short this pin to the ground and your machine should power up. Don't worry you wouldn't damage anything even you short every pin on the connector to the ground.

# Problem: 090

**I got a hp dv4-1220us. It has a full white screen on LCD, video on external monitor is ok. Found burnt Q43 on motherboard.**

## Solution:

That is a motherboard vga problem; you need to heat up the gpu chip on the motherboard

# Problem: 091

I've been having intermittent issues with my notebook where windows is reporting atapi and disk controller issues in the event log. At first I thought it might be a bad hard drive so I swapped it out for a new one but it's still coming up with the same errors.
I've noticed if windows get more than about 10 atapi errors in a row it drops the transfer mode from DMA mode 5 to PIO and then everything is very slow.

## Solution:

it is a disk controller issue on the notebook's motherboard, notebook's IDE controller can go bad.

# Problem: 092

What testers do you like to use for this? The first machine I purchased was a T862++ I just did BGA reflow I soon discovered this was not a reliable fix so I started reballing and/or replacing the chips. At this point I discovered the T862++ was not really suited to remove the chips (It may have been operator error) It seemed it would not get hot enough to remove them and when it finally did the chip was no good any longer. I had done enough work I bought a Jovy RE7500. It is working out a lot better. Next year I am going to purchase one theat has the x ray and thermal imaging. I also have a ESR/DSR tester a good volt/ohm meter.

## Solution:

My BGA rework station is low end one, for doing those lead free chips you need a machine has 3 temperature controllers, The one from top, the one from bottom, the one on outside area. And it must be very powerful. the one I use now is about 4800W. x ray and thermal imaging can't help you much and also is too costly.ESR/DSR is useless to diagnose problem, I have one but never used. Oscilloscope is very useful but not necessary. The Quata's best tech never use oscilloscope. But in the other hand, the best laptop repair man in China who becomes the top one in this field is because he is so good on oscilloscope to analyze problems. I will not say Reflow is not reliable; depend on what chips you encountered. For example, ATI vga chips usually can be done very well through reflow. Reballing is riskier than reflow, because you must heat the boards twice and chips 3 times. Removing BGA chips from boards must be the last thing to do – ONLY after you tried all other things and did all analyzing.

# Problem: 093

i have an old hp nx9010 laptop. while it works fine, it gets very hot. the region at the bottom next to the exhaust will be almost too hot to touch. the fan will spin at max speed a couple minutes after its turned regardless of what i'm doing. i have opened the case to have a quick look around but did not find much dust.

what is the likely cause/s of the problem?

are there any way to fix or alleviate this?

## Solution:

The vga is overheating , open the laptop change the cpu fan and add more thermal paste. Also ensure that the vent are not blocked.

# Problem: 094

Hi, I have a BenQ S42 laptop just recently out of warranty. I formatted and put Windows 7 Pro on it as I have done on many other computers but the day after, it stopped booting; it'd get stuck on a black screen with a blinking cursor.

## Solution:
Please rest the CMOS battery, it should fix the problem

# Problem: 095

Now the laptop works perfectly plugged in, it works fine on the battery BUT it doesn't recognize the battery even when it is RUNNING off the battery (says something like "not detected"). The bigger problem however, is that once it is not plugged in, the battery seems to completely discharge in about 5 minutes (was ~4 hours before this all happened).

What causes a healthy battery to complete discharge in 5 minutes? (fairly sure it's healthy..).

## Solution:

This is a circuit protection problem.

# Problem: 096

**Finally i try to replace PU7 MAX8743 , and surprise the mobo try to power up , i removed RTC battery before testing and now when connect the AC adapter the FAN automatically start and mobo try to boot but only have 0.7v at PL22 , maybe i overheat max removing from old mobo , when mobo try power up max8743 get a little hot ,**

## Solution:

Measure the resistance on PL22 PL23 you get 120 Ohms and 20 Ohms. Try also to replace PQ33 and PQ28 Now with the new max have present 3.3 v at LID_EC#.  The motherboard should power on .

# Problem: 097

**Please help....need to know if max8724 acok pin 11 (hp pavillion dv 9500 quanta at6 schematic) is an output of 5v out from max...or it is an input voltage..as i have 0 v (instead of 5v needed to gate for pwr on) ... and me with a Lenovo S10-2 netbook (same problem).**
**"Assuming" overheating caused a MoBo problem, what componet would be effected.**

## Solution:

acok it's an output voltage from max8724.....if it's  faulty...replace the chip

# Problem: 098

**Lenovo S10-2 netbook (same problem).**
**"Assuming" overheating caused a MoBo problem, what component would be effected.**

## Solution:

Mofets , Capacitors, fuse, transistors  chips on the motherboard will be effected

# Laptop Motherboard Component Overview

# Laptop Motherboard Ic identification

**Common Laptop IC Chip.**

**POWER SUPPLY CHIP** :- (MAX1632, MAX1904, MAX1634,SB3052, SC1402, LTC1628, TMP48U, ADP3160/ADP3167, ADP3168, APW7060 , ETC)

**IO CHIP** :- (PC97338, PC87392,FDC7N869, FDC37N958, LPC47N227, LPC47N267, PC87591S/ PC 87591L / PC 97317IBW/PC 87393 VGJ PC87591E ETC )

**CPU power supply chips** :- (ADP3166, ADP3170, ADP3421, AIC1567, CS5322, FAN5056, ITC1709, MAX1710/MAX1711/MAXl712, HIP6004 )

**Charge discharge control chip** :- ( MAX745, TC490/591, AAI3680, ADP3806, DS2770, LTl505G, MAXl645B, MAX745, MB3878, AAT3680 ,ETC)

**CPU temperature control chip** :- (MAX1617, MAX1020A, AD1030A, CM8500, MAX1989, DS1620,

**Graphics Brand chip** :- (ATI, NVIDIA, S3, NEOMAGIC, TRIDENT, SMI, INTEL, FW82807, and CH7001A

**Ethernet chips** :- (RTL8100, RTL8139, Intel DA82562, RC82540, 3COM, BCM440 LF8423, LF-H80P, H-0023, H0024, H0019, ATPL-119

**Sound audio Chip** :- (ESS1921, STAC9704, AU8810 ,4299-JQ, TPA0202 , 8552TS, 8542TS, BA7786, AN12942, AD1885, ALC655, APA2020/TPA0202

**PC Card Chip** :- (R5C551, R5C552, R5C476, R54472

**PC Card power supply chips** :- (TPS2205, TPS2206, TPS2216, TPS2211, PU2211, M2562A, M2563A, M2564A

**COM port chip** :- (MAX3243, MAX213, ADM213, HIN213, SP3243, MC145583

**Keyboard-chip** :- (H8C/2471, H8/3434, H8/3431, PC87570, PC87591

**Keyboard chip** :- ( H8/3434, H8/3437, H8/2147, H8/2149, PC87570, PC87591, H8S/XXX, M38857, M38867, M38869 )

**Battery IC chip**:- (BQ2040 BQ2060 BQ24700 BQ24701 BQ24702/BQ24703 M61040FP..)

**Memory control chip** :- (CM8501/CM8501CM8562)

**Clock IC** :- (CS950502 CY28404C ICS9248-153 ICS954218 ICS9248-151 ICS9248-39 ICS950901, WINBOND,)

**Lcd back light control** :- (MAXl522/MAXl523/MAXl524 OZ960)

**Ddr memory power supply** :- (MAX8794 NCP5201 SC1486/SCl486A SC2616 TPS51020 ISL6520, ISL6537 CM8501, ISL6224 ISL6225)

**Other Common chipset** :- (AAT3200 AAT4280 AMS1505, MIC2545, MIC5205, ADP3168, AICl567, cM8562, CMl9738, CSS5322, DSl620)

**Mosfets Used Crystal** (14.318 Clock )

**Connector Socket** (display, battery, dvdrom, modem, keypad, touchpad, onoff panel etc)

# Troubleshooting Laptop Motherboard Problems

**Laptop Motherboard Repair - Tips To Fix or Repair Laptop Motherboard Problems**

Okay it's time to talk about motherboards. Now I get the impression that motherboards scare a lot of people in this field, you know people don't want to deal with them or replace them or try to fix them. It's a little daunting to try to diagnose the motherboard it might seem, but what I'm going tell you is it's pretty easy. Here's four main symptoms that could go wrong with the motherboard and they are:

**Four symptoms of a bad motherboard:**

**1. Computer won't turn on**
**2. Components won't work**
**3. Computer shuts down randomly**
**4. Computer acts abnormally**

**1. computer won't power on.**

We got a laptop that doesn't power on. How can you tell if the motherboard is bad? Well, you just ask yourself why else wouldn't a computer power on? Number one, if it's on battery power, the battery is dead or the battery is bad and number two the AC adapter could be bad, so let's roll out number one.

Pull the battery out, keep the battery out of the computer for this test and then take your AC adapter and check the voltage with the voltmeter and I'm going show you how to do that right here. Take a voltmeter and what you want to test for is voltage. Put the meter at 20 volts DC and take the tip, the power jack tip. You hold your black, your negative on the outside of the tip and you put the red in the hole in the inside of the tip. Be very careful not to touch the red and the black and the tips together, otherwise it will create a short circuit. After doing these things, be sure you have 19 volts DC or just about 19 volts DC registered on your multimeter so we can know that the power adapter works. Now, just to make sure the connections is tight, kinda bend the power cord a little bit and make sure that the registered 19 volts DC on the multimeter or voltmeter will not fluctuate or move when you bend the power adapter cord a little. Okay if you're still getting 19 volts DC when bending the power adapter cord, jiggle the power adapter cord a little bit around make sure that there's no crimson wire. Now, after you bend the power adapter cord and jiggle it and you still have 19 volts registered on your multimeter, then the power adapter tip is probably good. A lot of time you know the tip will break, great in this area here, and you wouldn't get that 19 volts DC after you do that, after it's broken. So instead of just taking the whole computer apart and finding out if the laptop has appropriately good power jack, test the power adapter first.
Now another reason a motherboard might not turned on is because it's not getting power to the power jack. Power jack might be damaged, so absorb what you can from the outside and see if it's the power jack is loose or detached from the motherboard and if it is then you know you have to replace the power

jack probably, but if it looks like it's secure the only way we we're gonna be able to test the power jack is to get down to the motherboard level and look it where the power jack is soldered on to the motherboard and this I cover in many of the case study videos.

Other things that may cause a laptop motherboard not to power on...

Now there's a few other things that might cause a motherboard not to turn on or computer not to turn on, it could have a bad processor, but bad processor are fairly rare I would say 1 out of 75 computers are working on, it's the processor rather than the motherboard that's bad and also there's like maybe the power button on the actual laptop is broken or something mechanical like that, but again that's unlikely but you could check those things too.

## 2. Components won't work

Okay number two, components on a laptop won't work. For example, a CD drive or a wireless card don't show up in windows. Whether not working properly, well that could possibly be a motherboard but the way to test that is to replace that component. If your CD drive is not working replace the CD drive if it's still not working maybe the CD drive controller or the motherboard is bad. I've had that happened on a couple Toshiba laptops I worked on. I've bought a brand new CD drive put it in, still not working, still wasn't recognized by the BIOS and it was a bad motherboard. Now HP, I also had a problem of their wireless card but it wasn't the wireless cards that were bad it was the actual controller on the motherboard, that controls the card that was bad. I think it was positioned next to a chip that got real hot like the graphics chip or something like that, on the motherboard. So if you have a laptop with components not working, you replace the components and they're still not working then you might have a bad motherboard. Now how do you roll out if windows isn't causing this problem or the operating system's not causing the problem. Well, test it with a different operating systems. This is always a good test of the motherboard using like Linux distribution like knoppix or using the Ultimate Boot CD for windows. These are both bootable CD's and it's essentially testing the hardware of a laptop because you're running it on a different operating systems. Last thing to try if components aren't working and you suspect is your motherboard. Flash the bios of the motherboard, maybe the BIOS got corrupted somehow, and since the BIOS is like handles the basic functions of a computer, maybe it's not doing it's job and causing some abnormal activity in the computer.

## 3. Computer shuts down randomly

Okay number three, laptop shuts down randomly. Now this is a common symptom of a laptop overheating. So let's make sure it's not an overheating problem and how do we do that? Well, what I do is I take a can of compressed air and I blow it in the laptop, in the bottom where the fan is and also in the heat sink, on the side of the computer. If you do this you might see clouds of dust come out and that's a good thing that you want to make sure you get all the chunks out of the laptop before you turned it back on, because those chunks of dust that might still be stuck in there, might cause the fan blades to actually stick. I go over this in the case study videos several of them. Watch how I do that there and you can see in action you know cleaning out laptop, getting old dust out of it. Now, once you get the dust out of a laptop and you're sure that the fan is spinning and the airways are clean, if the computer keeps shutting down after this, you can be very sure that's not the CPU overheating that's causing the problem but the problem with the motherboard. I had systems where I opened them up I make sure all the airways were clean, I make sure that the heat sink was making a good connection with the processor, put it all back together and the computer still power down. It turned out it was a bad motherboard

## 4. Computer acts abnormally

Okay number 4, the computer or the laptop acts abnormally. It blue screens, things aren't working the way they're suppose to, it doesn't boot up every time, it doesn't boot up at all sometimes. Now, first I want to make sure it's not Windows that causing a problem. So again we're not going to deal to much for the software sides to do all your Windows fixes and make sure Windows isn't causing the problem or like I said before, just run knoppix which is a good Linux distribution, the Ultimate Boot CD for Windows which is also great and then you'll know Windows isn't the thing that's causing the problem then. If you're still having problems with the computer acting abnormally, start taking out components one by one. Take the hard drive out, you could do that if you're running it from a live Linux distribution. Take the ram out, replace the ram maybe with the stick around that you know is good that you have around in the shop, take the wireless card out take the CD drive out. Start taking components out one by one and get the motherboard down to basics like CPU, one stick of ram, motherboard and power, and hook up the screen, and just make sure that it goes on. But break it down to basics so you're sure that it's not a component that's causing the problem. So once you have it of broken down to basics and you're sure windows isn't causing the problem, then it's probably a bad motherboard. Okay it's a bad motherboard.

## Fixing dead motherboard power problem

## Dead Motherboard: Total Power Loss
### Laptop does not start. Is it bad power jack or power fuse?

Let's say your laptop does not start at all. You plug in the power adapter and press on the power button, but the laptop will not react. It's dead and the power or battery charge LED will not light up.

What could be wrong? Is it bad power jack or the motherboard is dead?

By the way, the power jack aka DC-IN jack is the power socket on the side or back of your laptop where you plug the AC/DC power adapter.

I'll explain how to perform basic troubleshooting and find out what is wrong. This is only for experienced people, who know how to disassemble laptops.

First of all, test the AC/DC power adapter with a multimeter. It's very likely that there is noting wrong with the laptop and your problem is related to the power adapter.

If the adapter tests fine and output correct voltage, disassemble the laptop and remove the top cover.

As you see on the first picture, in my laptop the power adapter plugs into the DC-IN power jack which is connected to the motherboard via a harness.
In some models the DC-IN power jack is soldered directly to the motherboard.

Plug in the power adapter and measure voltage at the point where the DC-IN jack or DC harness (like in my case) connected to the motherboard.

If you are reading the same voltage as on the AC adapter, it means the power jack or harness works properly and the problem is related to the motherboard.

If there is no voltage, most likely there is a problem with the jack or hardness and it has to be replaced.

By the way, in some case the problem could be related to the fuse which is usually located somewhere very close to the power jack/harness connector. You can test the fuse with a multimeter.

If the fuse is bad, the motherboard will appear to be dead even if there is nothing wrong with the power jack and AC/DC adapter. If that's the case, replacing the bad fuse should fix the problem.

## No power Problem
### Diagnosis, Cause and Remedy:

The first thing I did was testing the power adapter with a multimeter in order to verify whether the power adapter is the one that's causing the no power problem or not. The supply voltage indicated on the power adapter is 19v, when I tested it, the supply voltage is just normal. Since the power adapter is just okay, our concentration now is on the laptop itself. In order to ascertain whether the motherboard of the laptop or other peripheral devices which is connected to the laptop causes the no power problem, we have to disassemble the laptop piece by piece. After unscrewing all the laptop parts, I individually pull out each peripheral devices. After completely taking out all devices which is connected to the laptop. I now separated the motherboard in order to be tested. But first I clean out all the dust from the motherboard for this is also a one factor which causes the motherboard electronic components to be shorted. Because when dust gets thick it will become a conductor.

So you need to be aware of this, every time you disassemble a laptop motherboard you need to free the motherboard from all dust, to be sure not the dust is the element causing the motherboard's electronic component parts to be shorted. After cleaning all the dust from the motherboard, I scan all the components to see whether there are any dry joints or not. Dry joints means loose or poor solder connections. Poor solder connections on a laptop motherboard usually occur when your laptop is already well-advanced in years. I did not find any poor solder connections on any part of the motherboard, but for contentment I just carefully resoldered all the SMD components especially on the power section.

Note: All laptop nowadays is designed on a Surface Mounted Device or SMD mode, and this is rarely have dry joints. But for satisfaction I cautiously resoldered all the SMD components particularly the SMD components near the dc power jack.

After resoldering all the sections that needs to be resoldered, I inserted the dc power plug adapter to the dc power jack and see whether the power comes up. Unfortunately, the condition of the problem remains the same. I now tested all the electronic parts on the motherboard to find out whether there are any shorted electronic element parts which causes the no power problem. After testing all the components that could be tested merely with a multimeter, I could not find any shorted parts. The only parts that I still not checked was the dc power jack and the fuse.

The final step that I did was testing power jack from input to ground for short. When I tested it, voila! the problem found because it is really shorted. I used x1 range of my multimeter to see the fault and either way there's a deflection. When I go on testing the fuse, I found that the fuse was also open, the rate of the fuse is 5.5 amperes and upon further inspection I found a shorted diode.

The reason why the power jack terminals were shorted is because of the shorted diode that is connected to the power jack. Replacing the diode and the fuse brings the laptop to life.

## How to fix G4 Aple ibook motherboard

### G4 ibook motherboard fault.

There is a design problem with some G4 ibooks. It can appear after a year or so in some machines. After being on for a few minutes, they get a blank black screen, the fan turns on, and the computer freezes. This article describes the problem and how to fix it.

### What models are affected?

After doing this survey which involved over 300 faulty g4 ibooks it appears all models are susceptible to this problem.

The original 2003 ibook G4's (800/933/1Ghz) have the fault. The "Early 2004" (1Ghz) models up until Oct 2004 have the same motherboard.

The 60G (1.2Ghz) "Early 2004" model and all the "Late 2004" model ibooks (1.2Ghz/1.33Ghz) and Mid 2005 (1.33 and 1.42Ghz) have built in airport extreme which means a different motherboard but they still have the fault. Even models with the new motherboards are affected.

### What is the fault?

Here is a photo from the paper. You can see the thin black line below the lead which is a crack in the solder.

My ibook is indeed just as the article describes it. The little chip gets hot, and if I press my finger on the chip, it works! Take my finger off, it stops working!
I rang Apple Australia and they don't acknowledge that the problem exists. They have officially 'never heard of it'.

**The repair:**

You need to grab a fine tipped soldering iron and heat up the top few pins of the chip one by one to resolder it to the logic board. Press the chip down while you apply a very clean and fine soldering iron tip to each pin.

This is a very complicated 'how to' a bit outside the scope of this site but may be interesting to some. Don't attempt this one unless you have had lots of soldering experience!
Here are some pictures:

The G4 ibook with the bottom case off. The offending chip is circled.

Here is a closeup of where I have soldered the legs of the chip. You can see the base of the top pins are shinier from the new soldering. I soldered the top 3 or 4 pins on each side, but it's only the top 2 pins that the fault occurs with as they are the main power pins. I applied a little more solder to the joint as well, that's why it looks a bit lumpy.

# How to replace tiny sound ic chips in a Laptop motherboard

### Burnt ic chip on the motherboard

The laptop would not turn on.

Closer view of the burnt ic chip....

Bad chip needs to be replaced.

Learn how to replace bad ic chip on the laptop motherboard

IC chip is soldered to motherboard and the laptop now works fine.

if a chip is dead just replace it !!.

Advance ic chip removal process

How to remove ic chip with 102 pins.

1st) Remove the chip

The chip is removed then find the same chip from another motherboard.

Place Flux around the new chip in order to help with the soldering.

The contacts need to be free of solder so the pins can't short. Use the soldering iron to

brush away excess solder from the joints.

The old chip is removed. The new chip is now in place.

*Ensure that the version number on the old chip is the same as the new chip.

# How to install wireless card in an old Laptop motherboard

**Below is motherboard that needs a wifi card. There are 125 pins on the motherboard in two pairs. 250 pins !**

First solder the new slot in place.

Image below shows a soldered slot in place.

Now we just need a wifi card.

Ok the card is in place now this old laptop is wireless.

**How to remove tiny capacitor from Laptop motherboard**

The capacitor is removed and placed on the two penny piece.

Then replace the bad capacitor with a new capacitor and solder it to the laptop motherboard.

The new capacitor is soldered to the laptop motherboard.

[

## Checking Voltage and Short Circuits with Multimeter

Laptops aren't resistors, which is the short way of saying you have to think about what you see when you try to diagnose a laptop with a multimeter. One of the more useful tests you can do is to measure the resistance between the positive pin of the power input (usually the center pin of the connector) and ground. The outer shell of the connector is ground, but it's not usually possible to get both multimeter probes into the port without touching each other. Any exposed metal shielding on the outside of the laptop, such as the metal around USB ports, the video output, etc, should be connected to ground, which you can test separately. When you do find a good ground, the input resistance for a healthy laptop may be anywhere from a few hundred Ohms on up. Measuring on the 20K Ohm scale, this particular laptop read 6.48K Ohms. If you get a reading of just a few ohms or less, there's a short circuit.

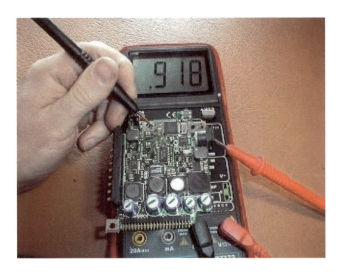

I'm testing the input resistance of a power regulator board. The connector on the bottom edge of the board married this daughter board to the laptop motherboard in the same plane. The connector to the left went directly to the battery bay connects. The input impedance of the board, reading 918 Ohms, was the same when the board was installed in the laptop, with the battery. Power regulation boards go for as little as $20 on eBay as pulls, and they can often be purchased new from Internet based liquidators on reasonable terms. The power board includes a couple of fuses that I'll get to on another page.

Testing the output voltage of an AC adapter is pretty simple, providing it's a standard barrel connect so you can get the positive (red) probe inside the barrel and use the ground probe on the outside, without taking any chances of touching the two probes together and shorting the output. The problem is, laptop AC adapters are switching power supplies, and they may require a load to start generating a voltage. It doesn't need to be a perfect load, and the multimeter may be enough. But, if you observed that the status LED on the AC adapter was lit when it was plugged into the laptop, and now that you've borrowed a meter and are seeing zero voltage, it's not lit, it's because it's not seeing enough load to fire up. Plug it back into the laptop for a moment, the LED will probably come on, and then stay on when you remove it from the laptop. The voltage should read a little higher than the voltage on the label.

The reading above is 19.8 Volts DC on a 19.0 Volt labeled AC adapter. If you've replaced the DC end on your AC adapter, be very careful when checking voltage. As mentioned above laptop AC adapters is that they are switching mode power supplies. While this gives them great advantages in low weight, low cost and flexibility on the input voltage, they may put out some audible high-frequency noise when not attached to a load, such as when the battery is charged and the laptop is turned off. As you can see in the picture to the left, the multi-meter probe is long enough to travel all the way up the inside of the barrel connector and possibly connect the ground. Unless you want to experiment with low voltage welding (AC adapter destruction) you don't want to create a short.

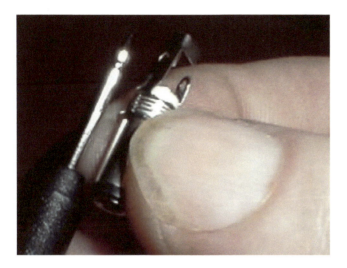

Manufactured (molded) cable ends are much less likely to be open, but there's no need to jam the multimeter probe all the way up the connector when checking the voltage. Another test you can do with your multimeter is to unplug the AC adapter from it's power source, the 110 V to 240 V wall socket, and look at the impedance at both ends. From the AC input, measuring between the recessed pins where the AC power cord would be plugged into the brick if it were powered up, you should see hundreds of kilohms (K Ohms), which means you have to switch to the megaohm scale to get a reading. If you get a beep on the continuity scale or a value less than an ohm on the 200 Ohm scale, it's a short circuit, and it shouldn't be plugged into live power. If you look at the impedance on the DC output side (this is still with no power), you should see a reading that keeps moving, as the capacitor charges up and the resistance increases.

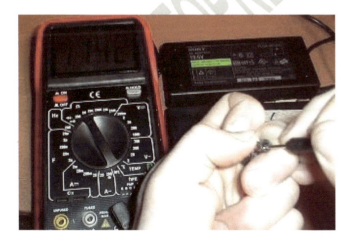

If you start on a high scale, 200 K Ohms or more, the reading might start by dropping and then stabilize at some number of K OHms, but if you start on a lower scale, you should just see the capacitor charge up and the circuit look like an open (over scale or a "1" on many meters). Again, if there's no resistance, it a short you can't plug it in until you resolve it. A short on the DC connector end is likely in the connector. And remember that shorting the output, even for a moment, will often fry the brick, so be careful with your probes!

## Testing for Backlight or Inverter Failure

I've been looking for an easy way to test for live laptop inverters for a couple years and I finally found a cheap, non-invasive method. The funny thing is I'd just ordered up a couple PC modding CCFL lamps with inverters to do a page about testing inverters with cheap replacement lamps. I'm not sure that would have worked given the impedance differences and the way inverters have to go through a timed sequence of voltage ramp up and down to strike and hold the plasma. Since the impedance drops when the tube lights and the plasma conducts, it's quite a bit more complicated than simply providing an RF power source. But as I was taking apart my old Toshiba screen today to expose the inverter leads for testing, it occurred to me to try the new Cen-Tech meter I picked up a couple weeks ago for $20. I'm showing the zero (well, 10Hz is well within 1% of zero on a 20KHz scale) reading with no power to the inverter.

Inverters put out fairly high voltage, in the 500 V to 700 V range, and a very low radio frequency, between 35 KHz and 60 KHz on data sheets I've looked up. That's something you could easily pick up with a spectrum analyzer and a probe for either the electric or magnet field component, but the last spectrum analyzer I worked with cost around $30,000, so it's a bit out of the reach of the home consumer. Now, the neat thing about the Cen-Tech meter is it comes with a Hz measurement. It's limited to 20 KHz, after which the display will simply show a "1" for over scale. Rather than equipping the meter with a special probe, I just held the two standard probes a fraction of an inch apart, and the son-of-a-gun picked up the cyclic field for the live screen almost an inch away from the inverter output, as shown to the left.

The weak signal results in a lower than reality frequency reading, and as I moved the probes close to the inverter output, it simply went off scale. I'd try to be more technical, but the instructions that came with the meter were so vague about its capabilities and what it's supposed to read that I'm just assuming here. The important thing is that the inverter test worked, and at no point am I touching the probes to exposed wires or terminals. This beats the heck out of a test I saw a guy recommending where he sets a multimeter to high voltage and shorts out the live inverter. He reported he could get a transient reading before the inverter shut itself down, and with luck, it would still work after rebooting a few times. The inverter is designed for an RF impedance, not to drive into a simple DC resistive load like a multimeter, and I wouldn't be surprised if that voltage test has ruined more than a few inverters.

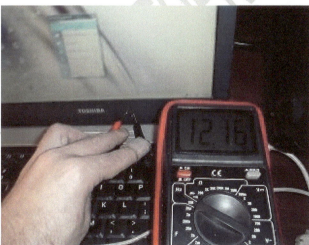

With my cyclic field test, I don't see how it can do any damage, unless you're careless with the probes and short out something in the screen. Then it occurred to me that the test could be truly non-invasive since laptop screens are so thin. To the left, I'm showing my newer Toshiba which I normally run plugged into a 19" Samsung monitor so I can see what I'm typing. A little hunting around on the outside with the spread probes and the meter picked up the field to the left. A further small move and to the lower left, you see the "1" indicating the field is off scale, higher than the 20KHz maximum frequency the meter can handle. Below, just as a proof, I'm holding the probes in the same spot with the laptop live, but the image diverted to the Samsung. Hunted around forever, no reading. So, this is probably the best use I've gotten from that MSEE I earned in the RF/Radar concentration 16 years ago!

Of course, into every test procedure some rain must fall, and when I went out and tested some other random laptops, as well as a simple CCFL tube and inverter for modding, my $20 meter failed to register anything! So I borrowed a better meter from my neighbor, a Fluke 110 true RMS meter. The Fluke specs show it's rated to 50KHz, which turned out to be critical in the inverter test application. As the measurment to the right shows, the Toshiba I'd originally tested has an inverter frequency of around 33 KHz. The reading varies a little with the exact positioning of the probes, the air gap, and the noise on the leads, but something in the sub 40 KHz was clear. That's why my cheap meter that is spec'd to 20 KHz was able to pick up the field, even though it was over range, it was still within an octave. But higher frequencies are just filtered out or unmeasurable.

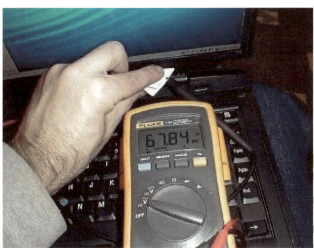

When I tested a Dell sub-notebook and my neighbors industrial rated laptop, I couldn't pick up anything on my meter. Using his Fluke, you can see that the inverter frequency was picked up as nearly 68 KHz. By this point, I'd taken to using a piece of paper to make-up the air gap, rather than trying to hold the probes apart. So I'm guessing the Fluke, which sells for a little less than $100 in the aftermarket, will cover all laptop inverter testing applications. The model 110 has been replaced by the model 115 which goes for around $110 new. If I have some time I'll design a little probe to function as an antenna, rather than just using the test probes, which involves a lot of fiddling around.

Of course, there are numerous things that can go wrong with laptop displays, so try to jump into testing the inverter before trying the obvious solutions. The first step, assuming you have power, etc, is to just plug in an external monitor and see if you can get that lit up. Newer laptops will usually autosense the presence of an analog monitor and shift the display without you having to use the function key (Fn-F5 on my Toshiba). If the external monitor works, you know that your video processor is good, that the laptop is booting into the OS, that the only problem is you can't see the screen. Wiring harness problems are common with laptop LCD failures because the screen is a moving part. The cables may fail in the hinge, or the constant movement and lid flexing may cause the signal connector to work loose of the LCD screen. It's also possible for the video connector to lift off the motherboard, especially if you're a heavy typer:-) When the external screen works, the cabling all appears good, and a very faint image is apparent on the laptop screen, you know that the backlight isn't lighting up. Not only is inverter failure more common than backlight (CCFL lamp) failure, but inverters are easier to replace. And now that it's winter, keep in mind that temperature has an affect on the voltage required to get the backlight to strike, so if the laptop has been sitting in a freezing car for a while and the screen doesn't light up, don't rush to take it apart. Give it a couple hours to warm up, but don't do anything whacky like sticking it in an oven or on a radiator!

## Testing A CCFL LCD Backlight Tube

Warning: Laptop inverters put out high voltage, usually between 500V and 700V, so don't try these tests unless you know your way around electricity. I'd also strongly advise against my sloppy approach of twisting wires and not even taping them.Since I recently did a page on testing a laptop inverter with a multimeter, I thought I'd go over some of the testing options for a backlight. Laptops employ CCFL tubes for backlights, due to their bright white light at relatively low power. Like all fluorescent lamps, CCFL tubes require a high voltage, high frequency input to strike a plasma and cause the tube coating to fluoresce. Someday not too far into the future, white LEDs should be available to do the backlight job with even less power and higher reliability. But in the meantime, a pairing an inverter with a CCFL is the way to light up a laptop screen.

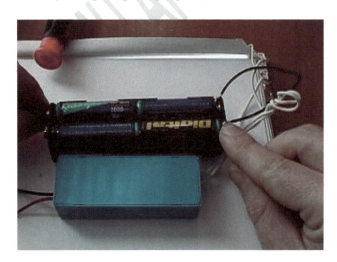

The picture above shows a 4" blue CCFL tube from a PC modding kit that cost around $3 by mail order. In fact, I think the shipping cost more than the whole kit, which included a dual inverter and the tube. Instead of using the PC connector provided with the kit, I cut the leads off and powered the inverter with 4 AA batteries in an 8 cell Radio Shack holder that cost $1.89. Since it was an 8 cell holder and I only wanted around 5V, I had to jumper the across the top, which I did by just sticking a piece of wire in the connectors. I also cut the output connector of the inverter since it was different from the connector laptop backlight I wanted to test. Then I remembered I hadn't tested the original modding backlight first to prove the inverter was functioning, which explains the first twist together job.

The picture above shows the modding inverter hooked up to the LCD backlight. I've folded up the white flap that covers backlight to help keep the light in the LCD assembly. The inverter did fire up the plasma, but not completely, which left me wondering if the CCFL tube was bad after all. However, it turned out that the inverter output was essentially linear with the input, as my neighbor with a variable linear power supply was able to demonstrate. I came back and put 8 cells in my battery holder and it fired the whole tube up. Unfortunately, I got the other four batteries by taking them out of my camera, so a picture was out of the question:-) Next I decided to try to fire up the backlight with the original inverter from the laptop. This inverter looked pretty standard and I guessed it would be happy on 5V, I know some laptop inverters take a 12 V input but I figured the lower voltage wouldn't hurt.

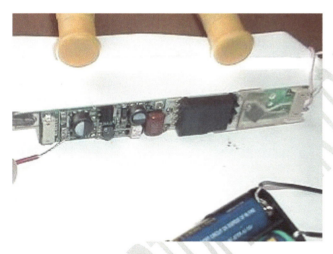

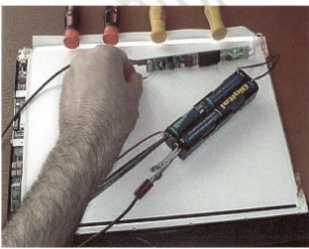

I'm simply touching positive lead of around 5V DC to the in-board side of the fuse, and you can see above that the backlight fired up at full brilliancy, even with the camera flash. I finally zoomed out so you can see that with the correct inverter, the whole backlight is lit up, and the light is in fact spread through the LCD substrate and visible at all the edges, as it should be. I had to take the metal back off the LCD to expose the backlight this way, which means that all the intermediate filters and layers wanted to fall out of the LCD if it was tilted. But it's much easier to tell what's going on from the back than the front, because in the "off" state, an LCD doesn't transmit much light, all the little crystal cells remain twisted closed. If you move the whole screen to a shaded area and fire up the backlight, the screen will visibly light a little, a sort of dull grey that's hard to capture with a digital camera.

To the right you see the LCD with the backlight lit full on, shot in the dark. You'll notice that there's actually more light leaking out the back of the LCD than transmitting through the screen. The lighting gradient you see is an artifact of the camera angle, the screen was even lit with a dull grey grid. Keep in mind that an LCD displays white by turning on the red, green and blue subpixels, which mix the light together for white. But the fact that some light leaks through when the LCD doesn't have any video input implies that for real black, the liquid crystals need to be twisted hard into an opaque state, their unpowered "off" mode allows some light to leak through.

## Recovering Laptop Hard Drive Files With A USB Shell

The worst thing that can happen to most laptop users, aside from the loss of the whole laptop, is hard drive failure. The hard drive holds all of your data, files, and all your e-mails and contacts if you use Outlook, Eudora, or any other non-portal based e-mail. But I'm sure many more laptops have gone to the recycling facility with live hard drives than dead hard drives. If you have any files you value on your hard drive that aren't backed up, you should invest $10 or $15 in a USB shell and attempt to recover the data. Hard drive data recovery is thought to be an arcane art, requiring expensive equipment and a high level of technical skill, but all of that only comes into play if the onboard electronics or the motor have failed. In that case, the drive platters are removed from the metal case in a special clean room, and the data is recovered by reading it off on a universal reader.

Most laptop owners are still very foggy as to where their data resides and consider the whole lower part of the laptop (everything except the screen) to be part and parcel with the hard drive. In reality, laptop hard drive are 2.5" wide, about 4" long and about a quarter inch thick. They weigh a couple of ounces, and can normally be accessed by removing a single screw from the laptop, as shown above. You should always unplug the laptop and remove the battery before attempting to do any repair work. I'll admit I left the battery in here, because I knew it had been stone dead for some six months or more, since the AC adapter died. After removing the single screw, you can see the 2.5" laptop hard drive installed in its cage. This hard drive is an IBM Travelstar, perhaps the most common hard drive used in laptops the past couple years. Because it's an older laptop, there's no shock mounting for the drive, little rubber washers that have become a popular way to partially shield the hard drive from the vibrations that can cause head crashes, in which case you can't recovery the data with a million dollar lab.

The series of pictures at the top of this page are for the older parallel ATA (PATA) drives, the <u>newer SATA laptop hard drive</u> is shown at the bottom of the page. The next step is to remove the whole cage from the laptop, which involves pulling back on the cage to free the drive's IDE interface from the laptop connector. You can see to the right that the drive cage is held from lifting by two metal tabs, and that the screw that held the plastic lid on the drive bay went all the way through and secured the cage in the laptop. That's all that held it together, one screw, and it's a typical arrangement. It turns out that removing the old hard drive from the cage, once it's out, is generally a bigger job than removing the cage from the laptop, because there are four screws involved and they are often overtightened and strip when you try to remove them. But it's not necessary to take it apart any further if all you want to to recover your old files.

I'm holding the new USB 2.0 interface that came with the $14.95 Sabrent hard drive enclosure. The interface is really all you need to gain access to the old hard drive, if it's healthy, and recover your data. The kit comes with software from Mac users as well as Windows based machines, but modern operating system versions don't even require the software. They'll just find the new USB hardware when it's plugged in, recognize that it's a hard drive, and allow you to recover your files as long as the file system types were compatible. I'm holding the interface card over the aluminum enclosure in which you could install the drive if you wanted to use it as a permanent external hard drive.

But when I started taking the screws out of the cage, three out of four fought me and the fourth stripped, despite the fact I was using a high quality screw driver. It would be easy to bend and break the remaining tab off to remove the cage, but why bother, when the only point of the job is to recover some old files? So I plugged the interface on (to the right), then set the whole thing down on my table with the new laptop and plugged it into the USB 2.0 port. You can see that the little green LED on the drive is lit and active, if you have good eyes and a better imagination.

Immediately after plugging in the USB cable, Windows XP picked up on the drive, and asks what you want to do with it. Choose "View with Explorer" and you'll gain access to all of the old folders, drag them onto your new laptop hard drive, and your data recover job is complete. Well, after you burn the recovered files on a DVD it will be complete, and you won't face the worry again. If the LED doesn't light up, you could be plugging the USB into an old port that doesn't source the 500 mA required, or the interface could be bad out of the box, or the drive could really be dead. If you don't hear the drive spin up, you can try picking it up gently, a few inches over the table, and try rocking in slowly to see if you can feel the centripetal force of the disk spinning.

In the 2005/2006 time frame, laptops started changing over from the older IDE (PATA) hard drives to the newer SATA hard drive. The only difference, as far as the user is concerned, is that the SATA drives are faster and have a different connector. The drives are otherwise identical, and the SATA drives often cost less in the larger capacities as they are more common today. Since the SATA interface only requires a few wires (serial vs. parallel bus), ribbon cables aren't required and a more flexible and robust connection is possible. The picture to the right shows an SATA drive installed in the laptop bay, and thanks to the rubberized shock mounting around the bay and on the cover, it simply sits tightly in place - no screws required. I only needed to remove one screw to take this drive out and put it into an SATA USB enclosure, and that was the screw on the drive bay lid.

Mounting the SATA drive on the circuit card for the external USB enclosure involves sliding the SATA edge connector into the circuit board connector and putting in a couple screws to hold it, if you're going to make the enclosure its permanent home. But don't make the mistake of thinking you're going to be able to boot your laptop from an external SATA hard drive, I haven't come across the laptop BIOS that can handle it yet. When the laptop BIOS gives you a "USB boot" option, it's the option to boot from a memory stick. Sabrent makes an SATA hard drive shell In any case, if your laptop is a brick and you need to recover your data, pulling out the hard drive and putting it in an external USB case is usually the easiest approach, providing that the hard drive itself isn't fried.

## Advance Laptop repair equipment & tools
**LEAD FREE FLUX & SOLDER**

**HOT AIR REWORK STATIONS**

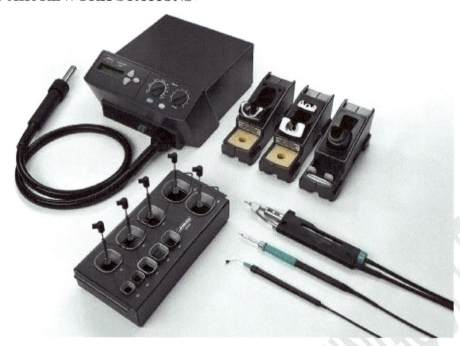

**BGA CHIP REBALLING AND REWORK**

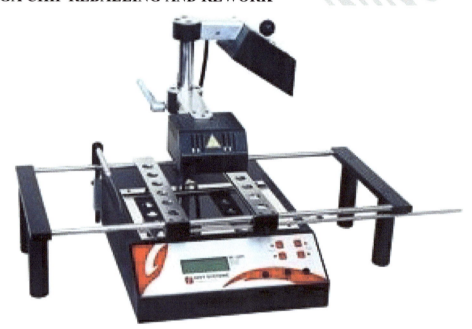

- BGA rework station,
- BGA ball making kit,
- 100 Mhz Duel Trace Digital Storage Oscilloscope,
- 400 Mhz Frequency Counter with PC interfaced Multimeter,
- 10 Mhz Function Generator,
- Duel Track Power Supply,
- Post Card Advanced PCI / Mini PCI / Express PCI,
- Universal ROM Programmer,

- Digital IC Tester, Analog / Digital R & D Breadboards,
- PTH De_Soldering Station,
- SMD Rework Station,
- Solder Bath,
- Micro Soldering Station,
- Microscope,
- Penscope.

# How To Fix Failed Nvidia Chip

This repair might apply to some HP/Compaq laptops and probably some other laptop brands.

**Most Common Symptoms**

1. Laptop turns on with garbled video on the internal laptop screen and external monitor.
2. Laptop turns on as normal but there is no video on the internal laptop screen or external monitor.

**Problem Description**

The NVIDIA graphics chip soldered to the motherboard. When the laptop gets very hot, the NVIDIA chip separates from the motherboard and laptop video fails.

**WARNING!**

There is no guaranty this method works all the time. While doing this repair you may damage the motherboard and make it unrepairable. Also, you may damage the laptop while taking it apart. Proceed at your own risk and don't blame me if you turned your laptop into a very expensive door stop. If you don't feel comfortable doing this repair, take your laptop to the repair shop.

**Fixing The Motherboard**

First of all, you'll have to disassemble the laptop and remove the motherboard. You can find laptop disassembly procedure in the course.

**HP Pavilion tx2000 laptop**.

In most laptops the graphics chip located under the CPU heatsink (and it has NVIDIA logo on it), so there shouldn't be a problem locating the chip. The chip has a glossy top surface.

For this repair I'm going to use an Ecoheat heat gun EC-100.

ECOHEAT Heat Gun
Model EC-100

In order to figure out how to position the heat gun and for how long, I tested it on a penny with a small piece of solder on the top.

The Ecoheat heat gun has a switch on the handle. There are two positions for the switch. Position 1 – slow. Position 2 – fast.
I used position 1 – slow.
I positioned the heat gun about 1 inch away from the penny and turned it on.

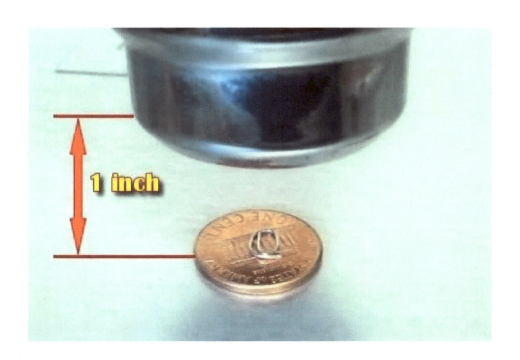

1 inch

After about 40-45 second the solder started melting. After 50 seconds the solder melted completely.

To protect the motherboard from the heat I used a regular cooking aluminum foil. I cut off a piece of aluminum foil and folded it a few times to make my protection shield thicker. After that I cut off a square opening right in the middle, same size as the NVIDIA chip.

After I removed the heat sink, I had some old thermal grease stuck on the NVIDIA graphics chip. You can remove old thermal grease using alcohol swabs. It's not necessary to make it perfectly clean. Just make sure there are no large chunks of thermal grease on the chip.

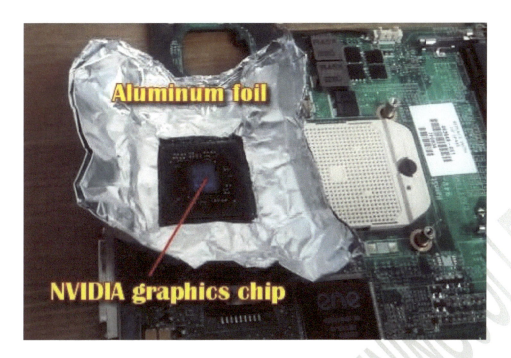

**UPDATE:** You can also apply some liquid flux underneath the NVIDIA chip for better results. I didn't do it this time. I'll definitely do it next time if the motherboard fails again

Finally, I positioned the heat gun above the NVIDIA chip about 1 inch away and turned the heat gun into the position 1.

After 50 seconds I turned it off and let the motherboard cool down for about 20 minutes.

Don't forget to apply new thermal grease on the NVIDIA chip when you install the heat sink.
Some laptops use thermal pads instead of grease. If that's the case with your laptop, make sure the thermal pad positioned correctly.

After I assembled the laptop back together, the video started properly!
The NVIDIA graphics chip problem fixed!
Will it last for a long time? I don't know. Still testing.

# DV1000/V2000/ POWER ON DETAIL

**First Step** is to check whether normal voltage VA is generated. (VA is the voltage through PJ1 Power Connector Adapter for Input Voltage.)If the Diode PD21, PD22 is open then VA voltage will not be generated in normal circumstance.

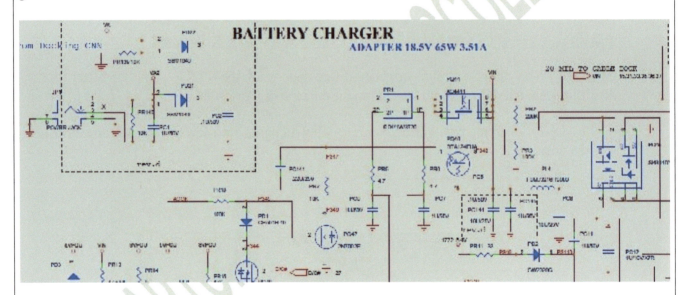

**Second Step** is to check whether the VIN voltage is normal. VIN voltage is the voltage from the VA conduction through the controlling MOSFET PQ44.

**Third Step** is to check 3.3/5 VPCU voltage is normal at Max 1999/8734. VIN voltage is generated as 3.3/5 VPCU in the basic premise of the system voltage. However, it only produces the two basic voltages necessary for the condition to up the power section.
Here, we take the MAX8734/1999 chip as an example :
1. Check whether the MAX 1999/8734 20 PIN has 19V input.
2. Check whether the chip's first 6 PIN SHDN has high 5V. When the pin is low, the MAX8734 /1999 will shut down and stop working.
3. Check whether the chip 5V-AL PIN 18 of MAX 1999/8734 generates a linear voltage. Here we have to note that the section of 5V-AL voltages should not be taken to mean 5VPCU voltage. As a linear voltage, it's current output is very small, which is available in the 3.3/5 VPCU voltage generator's start voltage before it. When the 3.3/ 5VPCU voltage stabilizes, the 5V-AL output PIN voltage will be 5VPCU and will take over to provide power. If the PIN has normal voltage

112

output, then we can say that the MAX 1999/8734 internal line is up and working. If not, with the exclusion of other chip pin under exceptional circumstances, consider replacing the MAX 1999/8734 power chip.

4. Now, check chip section On PIN 3,4 the ON3 and ON5 signal should be high.
The role of these two pins is to open the 3.3 VPCU and 5 VPCU voltages. If these 2 pins show low here then they certainly would not have 3.3/ 5 VPCU voltage.

5. Check 3.3/5VPCU output voltage, short circuit to ground to check impedance of the existence of such anomalies. If the voltage output is short circuit, MAX1999/8734 will soon be in line to protect their own state, to stop the output voltage.

6. Voltages examined on both sides of the MOS 3.3/5VPCU tube and connected to control circuit is abnormal. We can examine and control ON3 and ON5 pins.

Fig. System power main 5v 3v generate max 1999 schematic diagram

**Fourth Step** Check the Power Management chip, IO 87591L the first 44 PIN, the ACIN input pin on the motherboard. This voltage on this pin must be high. Also check the power supply of the adapter to the motherboard.

**Fifth Step** Press the start button on the power board, measure whether the power management chip's first 2 PINS (ON/OFF NBSWON) high to low transition is working normally.

**Sixth Step** Check the power management chip to detect whether the first 4PIN (DNBSWON to South Bridge) instant boot button is pressed. A high to low negative pulse transition should be detected. If not, then this is an indication of trouble in the power management chip.

South Bridge received DNBSWON low, it occurs SUSB #, SUSC # 2 high sent to 97551/87591, South Bridge chip part of the line is always in working condition. Likewise, it is also connected to a 32.768kHz Y5, its role is to South Bridge chip modules RTC and basic detection module reference clock.

Southbridge chip power management chip receiving the boot action to issue a pulse signal, this chip will be the first 26PIN the S USB #, the first 69PIN high of SUSC # set to an invalid state, the power management chip, boot up action to provide necessary conditions. parts.

**Seventh Step** Check to ensure that SUSB# and SUSC# pin is in the high state from south bridge received, . If one foot is in the low state, then it will be unable to achieve power management chip boot action.

97551/87591 received SUSB #, SUSC # after have had a SUSON, MAINON #, VRON. SUSON signals into SUSD signal sent tube arises 3VSUS, 5VSUS, and SUSON sent to MAX1845 generate 2.5VSUS.

MAINON # generated by PU7 SMDDR-VTERM. At the same time and by PQ119 PQ125 into MAIND send PQ143, PQ145, PQ148, PQ153 produce +3 V, +5 V, +2.5 V, +1.5 V voltage.

VRON gave PU9 (MAX1907), PU5 (1992E) generated VCC-CORE and VCCP voltage. PU6, PU4 signals generated HWPG to 97,551, then PU3, PU5 also various feedback signals to generate a HWPG 97551/87591.

At this point the M / B of the main voltage in each group have been OK back HWPG voltage feedback signal with convergence, the equivalent of a HWPG "and" relationship, such as including any group for the low feedback HWPG this POWER OK 97551/87591 occurs

Fig. :- 2<sup>nd</sup> stage power supply block diagram

**Eighth Step** Measure, with a multi meter, the SUSON (from I/O to MAX1845, on signals 2<sup>nd</sup> stage 2.5 1.5 volt ) power management chip149 PIN low signal, to see whether there is a high jump in the signal. This situation can be divided into two types: One is no action, the other is a jump, but without high maintenance of the signal. On focused inspection of input pin voltage, we can see that the signal generated is abnormal. The second case shows the power management chip to respond to the boot action and begin to work up. But unfortunately the control module voltage generates a problem, it cannot generate the corresponding voltage and the voltage OK signal back to the power management chip. In this case, the 63PIN HWPG (Power Good from MAX1845, MAX1999), under normal circumstances, should send a high signal to the power management chip.

When the power management chip to the PWRGD signal received after a certain delay period, to again PWROK signal to the corresponding delay circuit. Delay circuits at different delay, the order issued by the appropriate power supply OK signal. One, SB-PWROK signal to the South Bridge chipm NB-PWROK signal to the North Bridge chip. CPU-PWROK signal to CPU. Next, the system chipset will issue a reset signal, First issued by the South Bridge PCIRST # signal to the PCI bus and other related equipment and the North Bridge chip. Meanwhile, the North Bridge chip in the receiver to the South Bridge chip issued PCIRST # reset signal, we will send CPURST# signal to the CPU.

**Ninth Step** in the boot power, the ultimate PWROK signal, (which is sent to the North , South and MAX 1907 vrm chip). Power Management IC's **28 PIN** is the pin we are looking for. Generally, if the pin signal maintains a high signal, it indicates the boot was successful. The mother board's power supply module and voltage stability are maintained.

**Tenth Step** when the instruction to turn off opening of voltage, such as the OK is HWPG constant as high as 97,551, after receiving HWPG produce PWROK signal sent to SB Southbridge, Southbridge SB produced after the PCI RST # generated through U42 PCIRST # passed to North Bridge. North Bridge before they produce the CPURST #. Signal

## MAIN FOULT LIST WITH PARTICULAR ICS

**Main fault: MAX 1999/8743 3VPCU or 5VPCU bad output (usually board plug 19vin, there are two voltage output)**
1.   VIN_1999 input 19V voltage problems.
2.   Test 8 pin reference voltage is 2V.
3.   Check whether PQ103 PQ101 or bad.
4.   Measured with a Multimeter or 5VPCU 3VPCU ground impedance, small or short-circuit impedance for RMA board, the general line of parts for the burn. (PU10, PQ101, PQ103, PQ104, PQ102, PQ105, U23, etc.).

The IC is a voltage generated 2.5VSUS and 1.5V_S5 two groups, in 19VIN added after S5_ON, SUSON under normal circumstances, the two signals, that can generate the two voltages.

## Main fault: MAX 1845  2.5VSUS or 1.5V_S5 output bad (not voltage output and low).
1.   VIN_1845 input 19V voltage problems.
2.   Open bad.
3.   S5_ON, SUSON poor or no signals sent 1845IC.
4.   2.5 VSUS and 1.5V_S5 two smaller voltage-to-ground impedance or short circuit, for the RMA board, the general line of parts for the burn (PU5, PQ82, PQ99, PQ83, PQ106, PQ87, U16)

Signal description!
is the speed of the IC chip power management control, supply CPU CORE voltage, can automatically

correct the offset, ± 0.75% output voltage accuracy, a 0.700V-1.708V to voltage output range, 2V-28V power supply input voltage range and output over-voltage protection function.

# LAPTOP CHIP LEVEL TRAINING

**<u>Main fault: MAX 1907   Insert CPU no voltage output</u>**.

1.   VIN19V no input, PL12, PL18 bad.
2.   PQ107, PQ108, PQ109, PQ110 bad.
3.   5 VPCU not enter into MAX1907IC the 30PIN.
4.   Control signal VRON, SHDN, STP-CPU, DPRSLPVR, PWROK problems.
5.   CPU_VID0-5 signal not sent to the MAX1907.
6.   MAX1907
7.   Peripheral resistance, capacitance, diode and circuit problem.

Corresponding voltage generated the following way:

## <u>CONTROLLING</u>

1.   5 VSUS issued by PC97551/87591 SUSD signal to control PQ105 (4812IC), from the conversion over from 5VPCU

2.   +5 issued by PC97551/87591 MAIND signal to control PQ105 (4812IC), conversion from 5VPCU over the.

3.   3 VSUS: PC97551/87591 issued by SUSD signal to control PQ102 (4812IC), conversion from 3VPCU them there.

4.   +3 V: issued by PC97551/87591 MAIND signal to control PQ102 (4812IC), conversion from 3VPCU them there.

5.   +1.5 issued by PC97551/87591 MAIND signal to control the PQ87 (4800IC), conversion from 1.5V_S5 them there.

6.   1.2 V: is the +5 V through PQ113, PQ112, PU6B and 1845REF2V signal to control the PQ89 (4800), from 1.5V_S5 convert them there.

7.   VCCP is VRON by PQ91, PQ90, PU6A and 1845REF2V signal to control the PQ88 (4800), from 1.5V_S5 convert them there.

SMDDR_VTERM (1.25V issued by PC97551/87591 MAIND signal to control PU7 (LP2996IC), conversion from 2.5VSUS them there.
from the 97,551 issued S5_ON signals PQ73-PQ70-PQ70 parts produced S5_OND signal to control PQ100 the first 3 PIN, from 3VPCU conversion over the.

One main voltage: 19VIN: the total power input.
5VPCU: MAX1999IC generated.
3VPCU: MAX1999IC generated.
1.5V_S5: MAX1845IC generated.
CPU CORE: MAX1907IC generated.

Some of the main power is not the point of failure:
1. 0.001 A current fixed: generally 3VPCU, 5VPCU, 19VIN problems.

A current fixed: 3VPCU, 5VPCU, 19VPCU normal, 2.5VSUS, 1.5V_S5, +5 V, +3 V, 1.5V, 1.2V, 1.05V whether short circuit.

general short-circuit condition: 5VPCU ground short circuit, MOSFE tube, MAX1999 3VPCU ground short circuit, MOSFE tube, MAX1999, 97551/87591 chip.

On the ground a short Road, South Bridge bad.

To ground short circuit, Northbridge bad

A current fixed: 3VPCU, 5VPCU, 19VPCU normal, generally bad for the BIOS, 9 7551, South Bridge.

4, a plug power supply, current has been increased from 0.002A to zero a few amps, usually 97551/87591 chip burned. (97 551 poor, the temperature is high, hope the maintenance of attention, to avoid burns).

High-current, generally short, carefully measuring the voltage of each group on the ground impedance, replacement parts excluded failure.

POST self maintenance: self-test process

## POST self-test code table:

A system does not boot: DEBUG CARD run 00 of the state.
1.      The first of each group should measure the voltage supply is
2.      and then check whether the circuit and chip fat, warm, odor and other anomalies, timely treatment.
3.      E clock IC clock signal is sent to the pin on each chip.
4.      Measure the chip RESET signal is sent or received.
5.      Lace the BIOS.
6.      the main signal for the

    1). with empty CPU socket board installed in the machine, check the CPU to the      Northbridge Block signal impedance:

# 3-31 address signal, HD # 0-63 data signals, ADS address status, and control signals, determine whether the CPU and North Bridge air welding, poor

    2). North Bridge main signal check: HL0-10 South Bridge HUB bus interface connectivity.

## Memory does not boot: DEBUG CARD running 28, 38 and so on.
1.  Mainly the memory part.
2.  BIOS can also cause bad run of 38.
3.  The memory part of the main North Bridge Control: R_MD0-63, R_MA0-12, R_SM_DQS0-8, SM_B1-5, SM_CS0-3, M_DM0-8,
CKE0-3, CLK_SDRAM0-4 and other signals.
4.  In the inspection process must be carefully measured: North Bridge - exclusive group –
the memory slot of the signal, open circuit, short circuit and other undesirable phenomena.
5.  Check SMDDR_VREF reference voltage is normal.
6.  Northbridge, memory slots: empty and bad welding, welding or replacement material.

## Shown: DEBUG CARD running 59, 69 and so on.
1.  Northbridge peripheral circuits for voltage
2.  Northbridge bad.

3. Clock parts and clock IC bad.
4. U15, CH7015IC bad. FUNTION poor maintenance of the

# LAPTOP CHIP LEVEL TRAINING

1. Battery charge and discharge bad: PQ45, PQ44, PQ42 poor more.
2. 5 IN 1CARD bad: bad need of replacement slot; slot in the foot air welding; lines and for the voltage problems; PCI7411 chip air welding and bad need of replacement.
3. Bad: Interface bad need of replacement; 1394 24.576 MHZ clock is from the vibration; PCI7411 chip problem.
4. CARDBUS bad: Interface problems; PCI7411 chip problem.
5. USB bad: Line Interface problems; Southbridge bad.
6. LAN bad: Interface loose dirt poor replacement; U18IC impedance bad; clock could not afford to vibration; chips RTL8100 bad; around bad filter capacitor leakage.
7. MODEN and sound bad: MU2 chip bad; power supply; clock; amplifier and line. MU1 and peripheral circuits.
8. HDD bad: Interface circuit; Southbridge bad.
9. CD-ROM bad: Interface circuit; Southbridge bad.
10. KEYBOARD bad: bad interface circuit; Pai Yung CP1-6 poor; 97551/87591 chip, bad; BIOS program problems, need to replace the BIOS.
11. TOUCH PAD bad: bad interface circuit; 97551/87591 chip bad.
12. FAN bad: Interface, Q11, Q12, and the 97551/87591 chip bad.

## OTHER NOTES FOR IMPORTANT

Power management chips and BIOS chips, where 3.3VPCU, VC CRT C where normal electricity supply, will enter the working state. One-chip power management system can be understood as moments in the work of the monitoring status. Connected to the power management chip clock oscillator Y6 external power management chip to monitor the line to provide the basis 32.768kHz clock signal. If you do not have this clock signal, the power management chip will also be in a "paralyzed" state. -

Power Management IC 2 feet for the start signal to detect motion foot NBSWON #. Under normal circumstances, when the pin is detected over a negative pulse signal, the chip that was press the power button on the boot, and immediately turn signal through the first 4PIN of DNBSWON # "reported to the South Bridge chips."

South Bridge chip part of the line is always in working condition. Likewise, it is also connected to a 32.768 kHz external when Zhong Jingzhen Y5, its role is to South Bridge chip modules RTC and basic detection module reference clock.

Southbridge chip power management chip receiving the boot action to issue a pulse signal, this chip will be the first 26PIN the S USB #, the first 69PIN high of SUSC # set to an invalid state, the power management chip, boot up action to provide necessary conditions.

Parts.

Power management chip in the receiver to the South Bridge chip SUSB #, SUSC # control signal "Reply" In the future, it began to issue secondary power control signal (S5-ON, SUSON, MAINON, and

VRON) to each computer motherboard chip supply voltage generated. 3 N3 j8 H1 z I1 Z

# LAPTOP CHIP LEVEL TRAINING

DC / DC power supply generating circuit will have all the appropriate supply voltage to achieve stability in their output will be issued PWRGD high effective signal back to the power management chip, meaning that tell it, had now been given the task of successfully completed. Next, the power management chip control chip can be reported to the superior work.

When the power management chip to the PWRGD signal received after certain

delay period, to again PWROK signal to the corresponding delay circuit. Delay circuits at different delay, the order issued by the appropriate power supply OK signal. One, SB-PWROK signal to the South Bridge chip, NB-PWROK signal to the North Bridge chip, CPU-PWROK signal to CPU. Next, the system chipset will issue a reset signal, first issued by the South Bridge PCI RST # signal to the PCI bus and other related equipment and the North Bridge chip. Meanwhile, the North Bridge chip in the receiver to the South Bridge chip issued PCIRST # reset signal, we will send CPURST # signal to the CPU. check sequence:;)

South Bridge, the main signal checking: AD0-31 composite address data signal line, C/BE0-3 bytes to allow the signal line, the control signal line, LAD0 -3 + LDRQ0 + LFRAME # even the case in which the hard disk access 97,551 chips in the LPC bus interface.

4). MINI PCI slot on the PCI bus can be measured to check the appropriate bus plug-in circuit.

5). 97 551 chip, the signal inspection: LAD0-3 + LDRQ0 + LFRAME # signal.

6). BIOS checks on the signal: A0-19 address lines, D0-7 data lines, CS # chip select signals, RD # read the signal, WR # write signal and power ground.

7). try to make it clear fault region, to facilitate maintenance.

If the above does not find problems, from the perspective of poor parts replacement parts to repair.

www.ingramcontent.com/pod-product-compliance
Lightning Source LLC
Chambersburg PA
CBHW041418050326

40689CB00002B/567